Fly Fishing Midwestern Spring Creeks

angler's guide to trouting the driftless area

ROSS A. MUELLER

GOOD THINGS TO KNOW

First Edition

ISBN: 0-9648047-1-9

Library of Congress: 99-068466

Published by R. Mueller Publications
400 South Court
Appleton, WI 54911

Printed by Palmer Publications, Inc.
PO Box 296
Amherst, WI 54406

Photographs and illustrations by author unless otherwise noted.

Photo credits: back cover, upper photo, Paul Mueller;
back cover, lower portrait, Lois Mueller.

All trout photographed were released.

To all friends
of our spring creeks.

CONTENTS

ACKNOWLEDGMENTS

A special thanks to my wife Lois for her much-needed administrative and computer assistance.

To Dana Zimmerman for invaluable typing, editing and proofreading assistance.

To Chuck and Roberta Spanbauer, Heidi Bittner-Zastrow, Regina Paschall, Nancy Miller, Marcia Lorenzen, Connie Halverson and the staff at Palmer Publications for their professional expertise in the production of this book.

To the fly-fishing "pros" who have contributed to this book: Wayne Bartz, Walt Coaty, Tom Dornack, Mike Hogue, John Shillinglaw, Bill Stark, Dick Ward, Tom Wendelburg and Norm Zimmerman. Thanks again to Norm for manuscript advice.

To Mark Ebbers of the Minnesota DNR, Dave Moeller of the Iowa DNR and Dave Vetrano of the Wisconsin DNR for valuable trout stream information.

To Tom Andersen for fly-fishing equipment considerations.

To Bob Braendle and Pat Murray for photographic advice and to Paul Mueller and Fred Young for streamside photo assistance.

To Steve Davies, Mary Swab and Dave Knipfer of Mapping Specialists Limited, Madison, Wisconsin.

To John van Vliet for publishing advice.

PREFACE

The Driftless Area of the upper Midwest is a unique geologic region. It is an unglaciated area of ridges, valleys and spring creeks encircled by rolling, glaciated country. As a well-defined geologic region, it is like the Black Hills, which is an area of regional uplift surrounded by plains.

The trout-holding spring creeks of the Driftless Area (also known as the coulee country or bluff country) are becoming well known to fly anglers. Various fly-fishing publications have described portions of the Driftless Area. *Fly Fishing Midwestern Spring Creeks, an angler's guide to trouting the driftless area* explores the entire region from a fly-fishing perspective. This book is not a stream-by-stream guide but instead presents "good things to know" about fly fishing any stream of the region. This knowledge will be of value on spring creeks everywhere.

Although some fly patterns from my first book, *Upper Midwest Flies That Catch Trout and how to fish them*, reappear, many new stream-tested patterns are presented. Such hatches as the "tiny olives" and crane flies are covered in more detail, while hatches that have been heavily exposed in books and articles receive more limited discussion. Reader familiarity with trout stream insects is assumed.

Some streams located just beyond the boundaries of the Driftless Area are included because of their importance to the fly fisher.

As with my first book, I have relied extensively on my streamside notes for information. I hope the fly angler will find in this book many "good things to know."

INTRODUCTION

The upper Midwest contains a vast domain of limestone spring creeks. This area, geologically known as the Driftless Area, encompasses portions of southwest Wisconsin, southeast Minnesota and northeast Iowa (see map on page 2). This region contains one of the world's greatest concentrations of limestone spring creeks. With more than 600 streams of 2,500 miles of water, the Driftless Area may be compared to the chalk stream region of England, the limestone country of Pennsylvania and the spring creek valleys of the American West. Most of the Driftless Area streams hold trout.

The Driftless Area is an "island" of land that is geologically different from the surrounding land. This region was largely unglaciated or only lightly touched by the glaciers, leaving the layered, gently sloping sedimentary rock undisturbed rather than "bulldozed." The name *Driftless* refers to the absence of glacial deposits, or "drift," in this area. The intact layers of sedimentary rock were deeply eroded by streams, resulting in the characteristic ridge/valley configuration known as the "bluff country" or "coulee country." The Mississippi River bisects the entire region. All the spring creeks drain into the Mississippi either directly or indirectly via larger tributaries, such as the Zumbro, Whitewater or Root of Minnesota; the Upper Iowa and Turkey of Iowa; and the Trempealeau, La Crosse, Wisconsin, and Grant of Wisconsin. Even the Rock River of Illinois drains multiple Wisconsin spring creeks. Fortunately for the fly fisher, the geologic configuration of this area is ideal for the production of quality spring creeks.

Geologic conditions necessary for the production of spring creeks include favorable soils that allow surface infiltration of rain water, porous and sloping bedrock that allows percolation and flow of groundwater, and discharge points (springs) that occur where the water table is exposed at the surface.

These geologic conditions occur in the Driftless Area (see Diagram 1). The unglaciated soils, mainly sandy and silty loams derived from dolomite and sandstone, allow rainwater infiltration. The bedrock underlying these soils consists of a layer of dolomite (limestone with a high magnesium content) overlying older sandstone formations. These strata are permeable and inclined, allowing groundwater percolation and flow. Outcrops of this bedrock are often seen on the steep valley walls. If you have ever walked a bicycle through the tunnels of the Elroy-Sparta bike trail, you've experienced the sandstone aquifer; it is cool (about 50° F) and drips water.

The Driftless Area.
    The Driftless Area is an unglaciated area of ridges, valleys and spring creeks encircled by glaciated terrain.

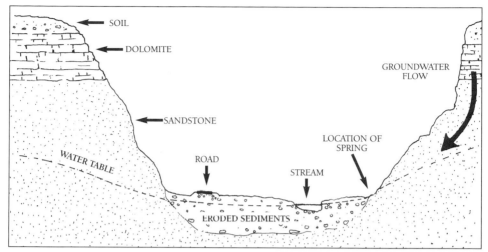

Diagram 1—Cross section of a Driftless Area ridge/valley/stream.
Rainfall infiltrates the surface soil, then percolates and "flows" as groundwater through the dolomite and sandstone bedrock. (Calcium and magnesium carbonates are dissolved into the groundwater from the dolomite). The zone below the dotted line (water table) is saturated with water. Springs and streams appear wherever the water table is exposed at the surface. Surface "runoff" of rainfall also contributes nutrients.

A distinction may be made between the spring creeks of the Driftless Area and spring creeks of other regions of the Midwest. The Driftless creeks are "limestone," or "alkaline," streams because of the dissolved calcium and magnesium carbonates derived from groundwater percolating through the ridge-top dolomite, a condition lacking in the geology of non-Driftless spring creeks, such as Lawrence Creek, the Brule, Au Sable and others that originate from the groundwater of glacial deposits. Glacial topography is rolling terrain because the hills have been flattened and the valleys filled.

The steep ridge/valley configuration of the Driftless Area accounts for strong discharge of groundwater as springs because the deeply-eroded valleys cut right into the water table. Artesian conditions, or groundwater under sufficient pressure to force it from soil or rock above the water table, are common. One cannot spend a day astream without seeing or hearing many springs and feeders (see Color Plate 2). Most are small, but some can be fished right at their exit from the sandstone.

Conditions for the production of cold-water alkaline streams are well satisfied in the coulee country, and most streams provide the necessary habitat requirements for trout: water temperature, protective cover, food supply and reproductive conditions.

Brook trout cannot survive prolonged water temperatures over 77° F, brown and rainbow trout slightly higher. Optimum temperatures for trout feeding and

3

growth are in the low to mid-60s. Brown and brook trout eggs and fry have high winter mortality if water temperatures approach freezing. Optimum water temperatures for trout, relative to our Midwestern climate, mean warm water in winter and cold water in summer. The strong year-round groundwater flow of the coulee country, at 48° to 50° F, provides the stability of temperature that trout require.

Aquatic plants and microorganisms, vital links in the food chain of the trout, depend on sunlight, oxygen and stream "fertility." The alkaline nutrients are important for the development of aquatic vegetation, just as a lime-rich garden soil is important to various garden plants. An alkaline environment, rather than acidic, benefits Baetis and many other insects that are important to the fly fisher: scuds, cress bugs and crayfish utilize the calcium for their exoskeletons. Fertility is further increased by vegetative material either directly deposited in or carried to the stream by runoff. A limestone spring creek has a faint but noticeable blue-green color.

Conditions for the reproductive success of brown and brook trout, which spawn in fall, are favorable in many streams with good supplies of gravel for redds and oxygen-rich, silt-free groundwater sources for egg and fry development (see Color Plate 2). Some streams are "trout factories," allowing transfer of wild coulee trout to streams of other regions. If you follow an electrofishing stream survey crew, you will be amazed by the truly great numbers of trout present in many of our streams (see Color Plate 3).

The appeal of the Driftless Area is not limited to the streams and the trout. This beautiful region is predominantly rural with the ridge tops and flat valley bottoms suited to agriculture. The steep sides of the valleys are wooded. Whether standing on a ridge top looking down or in a valley looking up, you will be impressed by the natural wooded bluffs with outcrops of bedrock (see Color Plate 3). Sometimes the walk back to the car after a session on the river is as enjoyable as the fishing itself (see Color Plate 4). In summer you'll notice the fragrance of wild mint; in fall, the aroma of freshly cut tobacco.

The coulee area streams offer a variety of fishing environments. If you prefer, choose a pasture with no casting challenges or the brush with many casting hazards; choose a small, high-gradient headwater stream or a large, slow river miles downstream.

It also is easy to roam around on our streams because miles of public water are accessible by either fishing easements or government-owned land. On private stretches, most landowners allow access if fishing permission is asked.

Fishing is available all year where regulations permit (see later). In addition, I appreciate being able to fish all day; there is no need to wait until evening to enjoy success as is so often the case on streams of other regions.

The stream locations are concentrated, and traveling from one stream to another is usually easy. For instance, the drive from French Creek in Iowa to Bohemian Valley in Wisconsin takes little more than an hour and is enhanced by sights of the Great River Road along the Mississippi. This convenience differs from the Western experience, in which traveling from one stream to the next is often a 250-mile trek.

Added to the unique combination of beauty, availability, variety and convenience is an emotional appeal. You will often have the feeling you've gone back in time a bit. "Coon Valley—what America used to be," reads the bumper sticker. Some uncrowded counties in the region have as few as two traffic lights. Oncoming drivers on back roads often wave. I hope that the area stays that way.

A period of severe degradation of coulee country streams began 150 years ago, when early settlers cleared native forests of trees for lumber and cleared the prairies for agricultural use. Subsequent grazing and plowing of these cleared areas contributed to run-off of rainwater instead of infiltration into groundwater. Flood erosion and sedimentation followed, along with diminished discharge from springs. Water temperatures increased.

By 1900 the abundant native brook trout were nearly eliminated because of overfishing and habitat destruction. The Minnesota trout management report "A Review of Trout Management in Southeast Minnesota Streams" mentions an individual who, in the 1880s, took 72 brook trout in two hours on Little Pickwick Creek (see References). Stocking programs began with brook trout and the introduction of brown and rainbow trout. However, put-and-take stocking persisted for decades in combination with low populations of wild fish.

"It is easy to roam around on our streams because miles of public water are accessible by either fishing easements or government-owned land."

Introduction

In the 1930s, government agencies were created to improve agricultural practices. For erosion control, soil conservation programs were implemented: contour plowing, rotational grazing, flood-retarding coffer dams and stream-bank repair. State conservation departments purchased lands for parks, forests and wildlife. Instream habitat improvements targeted specifically for trout began in the 1940s. At that time, former stream degradation trends gradually reversed, decreasing flooding and erosion, increasing discharge from springs and extending cold water downstream.

By the 1970s, instream habitat improvement projects became a major trout management focus, particularly provisions for enhancing spawning areas, fencing cattle and providing overhead cover.

The Departments of Natural Resources of Wisconsin, Minnesota and Iowa base current management strategies on ecosystems. Broadly based multi-agency watershed programs and instream habitat improvements are keys. Others include stream assessments and research, angler surveys and regulation, public access acquisition through land purchase and fishing easements, stocking considerations, educational programs and more. Areas accessible to the handicapped have been provided.

The Iowa trout program has been dependent on some kind of stocking, principally supported by put-and-take planting of catchable-sized trout because of limited natural stream reproduction. In the 1960s, stocking of fingerling trout was instituted in private waters (put-and-grow) to allow anglers the opportunity to catch stream-reared trout in a more solitary environment. Special regulations have been added in recent years on streams with self-sustaining trout populations.

Dave Moeller, supervisor of Iowa's Northeast Regional Fisheries, in a personal communication states, "We are very encouraged in recent years to see many more streams develop at least some natural reproduction, with several being totally self-sustaining."

Iowa's most recent trout angler survey revealed nonresident trout stamp sales to be over 10%, an all-time high. Special regulation fisheries have increased in popularity. Anglers fishing primarily with flies have increased, while those using primarily bait have decreased. Increased habitat improvement was the most frequently mentioned recommendation for improvement of the trout program. A program to preserve wild brook trout has been initiated, using fish that may be from a native remnant population (see References).

Mark Ebbers, trout and salmon program coordinator of the Minnesota Department of Natural Resources, notes that stream surveys in southeast Minnesota have revealed encouraging trends in that state's trout management program. Trout reproduction during the last 30 years has increased dramatically because of improved land management and improved instream habitat. Miles of streams supporting trout in southeast Minnesota have increased from 281 in the 1970s to more than 700 in the 1990s. The number of brown trout greater than 12 inches has increased two- to-threefold in the past quarter century and is still increasing, yet the number of fish over 15 inches has not increased. Efforts to increase this number by special regulations and to improve instream habitat are being undertaken. Over three miles of stream habitat restoration is being added annually. Average annual angling pressure has increased from 330,000 hours in the 1940s to 1,130,000 hours in the 1990s, based on an increase of 288 miles of managed water during the period.

"Wisconsin's trout management programs set an example of habitat steward-ship that other states should emulate," notes the recent Trout Unlimited report "Status and Trends for Inland Trout Management in Wisconsin" (see References).

Dave Vetrano, fisheries biologist of the West Central Region of the Wisconsin Department of Natural Resources, notes that southwestern Wisconsin streams had a small amount of brown trout reproduction in the late 1970s. By the late 1980s, however, an "astronomic" increase had occurred, again because of improved land use and increased trout habitat. Brown trout are now doing well "on their own" and are appearing naturally in streams in which they previously had been absent. An active wild brook trout program is restoring "brookies" to their former habitat.

Habitat restoration efforts are improving approximately 8 to 10 miles of water each year in southwestern Wisconsin. Important to this restoration are "lunker" structures, instream rock and logs, and the narrowing of headwater streams to expose gravel for spawning by increasing current velocity.

Private organizations and individuals have made significant contributions to our spring creeks. An important example is the Trout Unlimited "Home Rivers Initiative," launched in 1996 and described in "A Toehold in the Kickapoo" (see References). The scope of the project is the entire Kickapoo watershed with its 280 miles of cold-water streams, and the goal is to improve the health of the watershed. Key components of this three-year $500,000 project include watershed research, planning, restoration and education. Additionally, demographic and fishery infor-mation is being gathered. Groups such as state and local Trout Unlimited chapters, West Fork Sports Club and other regional sports clubs, school groups, county land conservation services, the University of Wisconsin and the Wisconsin Department of Natural Resources have been active.

Since 1981, members of the Hiawatha Chapter of Trout Unlimited in Rochester, Minnesota, have volunteered over 12,000 hours working on stream improvement projects in that area. Over $250,000 has been spent on these restorative efforts.

Contributions by 1,000 Friends of Wisconsin and Trout Unlimited have been used for multiple stream improvement projects in southwest Wisconsin.

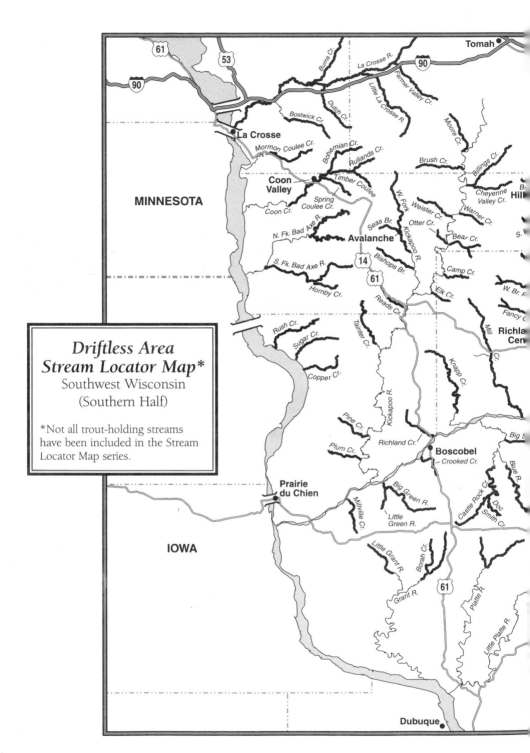

**Driftless Area
Stream Locator Map***
Southwest Wisconsin
(Southern Half)

*Not all trout-holding streams
have been included in the Stream
Locator Map series.

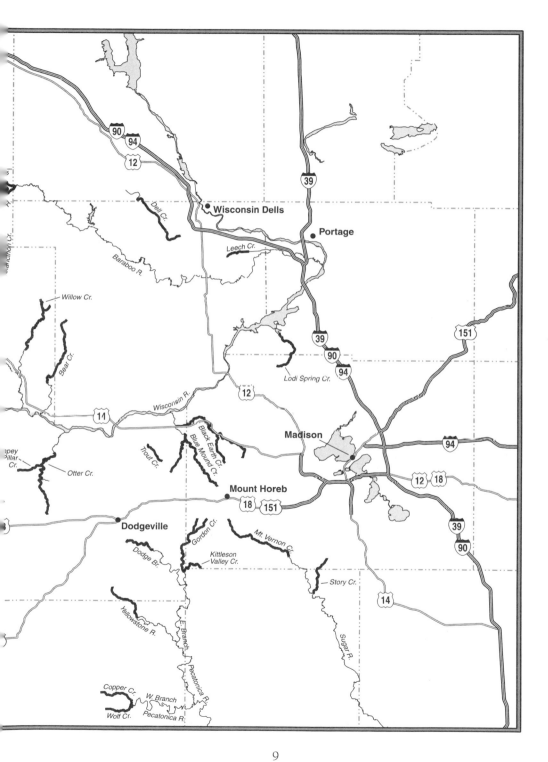

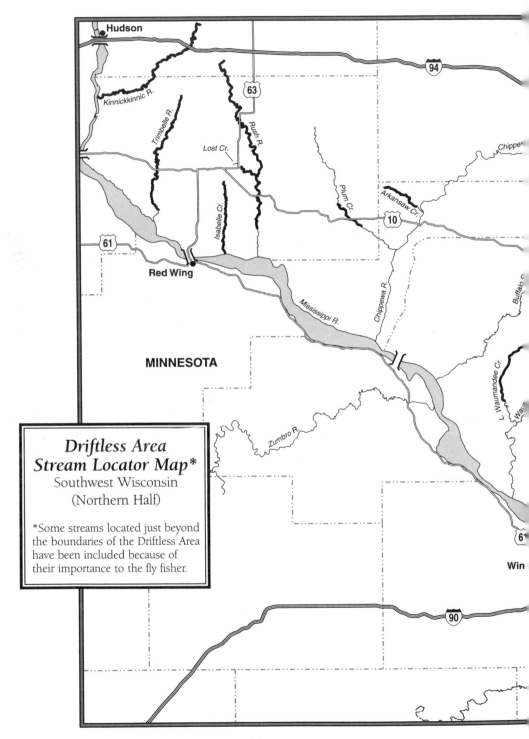

Hudson

94

63

Kinnickkinnic R.

Trimbelle R.

Lost Cr.

Rush R.

Plum Cr.

Arkansaw Cr.

Chippe

10

61

Isabelle Cr.

Red Wing

Chippewa R.

Mississippi R.

Buffalo

MINNESOTA

L. Waumandee Cr.

Wau

Zumbro R.

Driftless Area Stream Locator Map*
Southwest Wisconsin
(Northern Half)

*Some streams located just beyond
the boundaries of the Driftless Area
have been included because of
their importance to the fly fisher.

6

Win

90

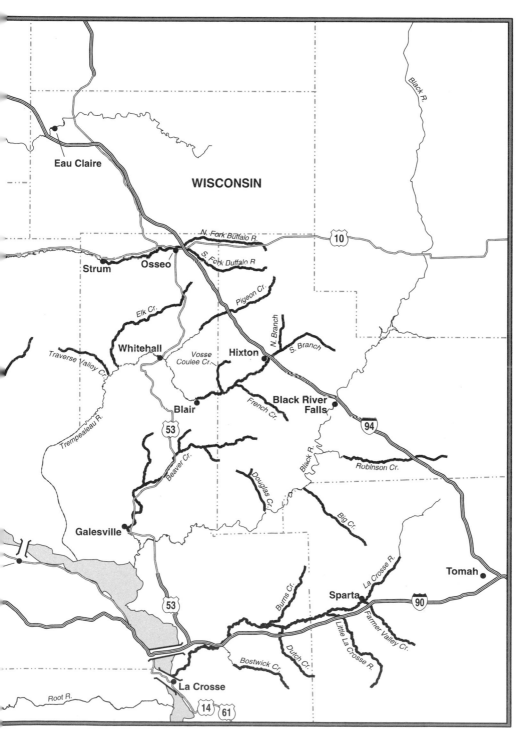

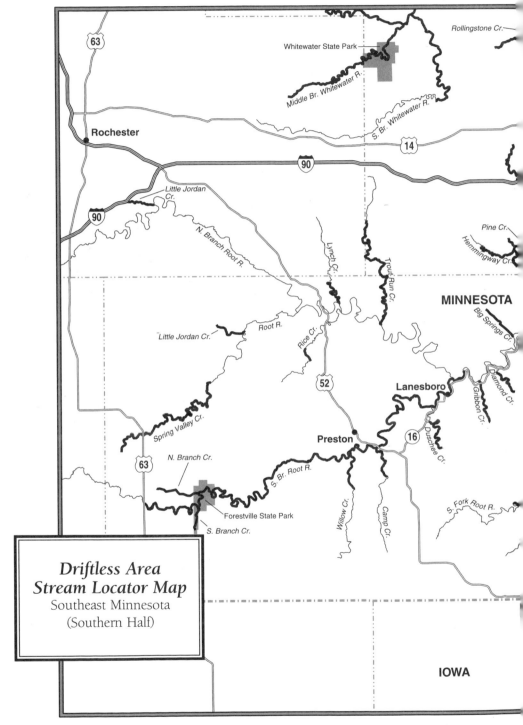

**Driftless Area
Stream Locator Map**
Southeast Minnesota
(Southern Half)

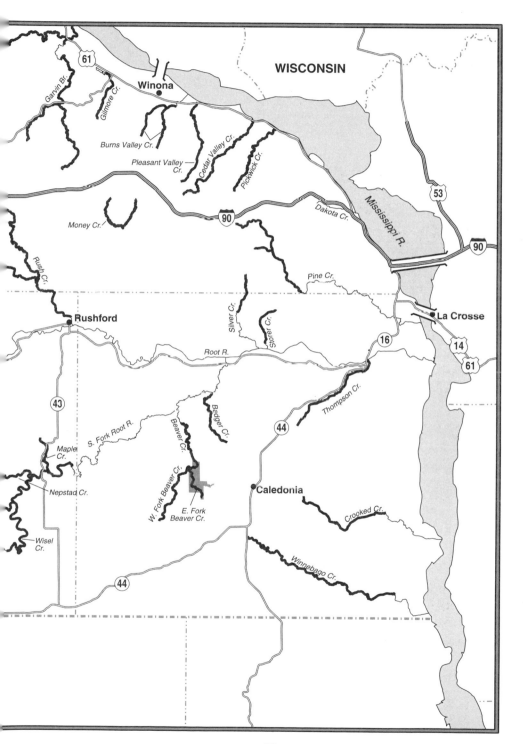

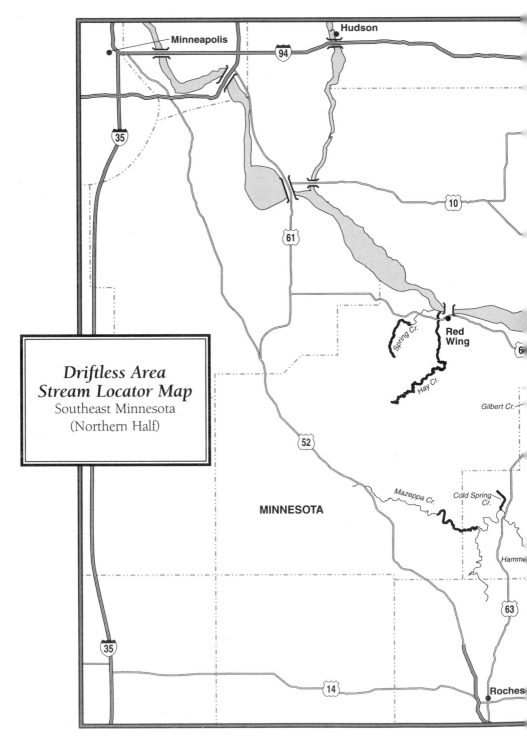

**Driftless Area
Stream Locator Map**
Southeast Minnesota
(Northern Half)

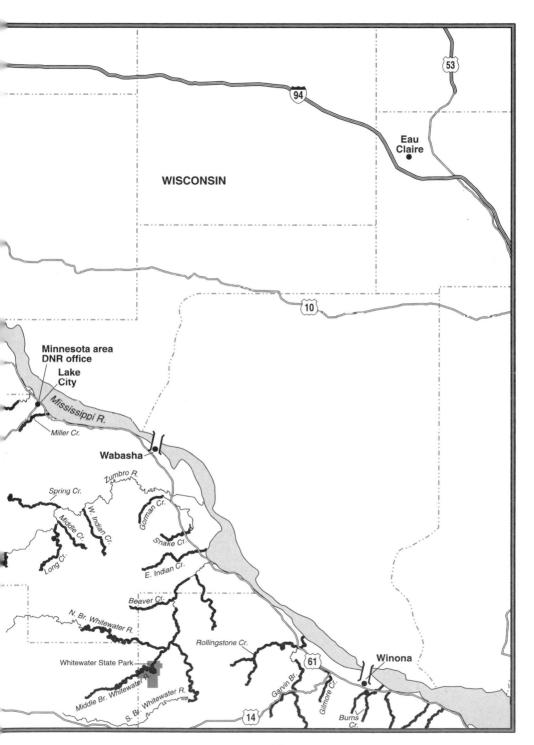

MINN.

● **Rushford**

● **La Crosse**

(16)

● **Caledonia**

(14)

(61)

● **De Soto**

Coldwater Cr. (52) *Mid. Bear Cr.*

Waterloo Cr.

Clear Cr.

Upper Iowa R.

WISCONSIN

(14)

S. Bear Cr.

N. Bear Cr.

W. Canoe Cr.

S. Pine Cr.

Patterson Cr.

Coon Cr.

Silver Cr.

French Cr.

Lansing

Clear Cr.

Erickson Br.

(61)

Decorah

Twin Springs Cr.

Trout Run Cr.

(76)

Waukon

Wexford Cr.

Paint Cr.

Little Paint Cr.

Decorah Rearing Station

Teeple Cr.

Hickory Cr.

Yellow River State Forest

Prairie du Chien

Big Spring Rearing Station

Bloody Run Cr.

(52)

McGregor

Turners Cr.

(18)

Glovers Cr.

Turkey R.

Sny Magill Cr.

N. Cedar Cr.

(18)

Otter Cr.

Buck Cr.

(61)

Mink Cr.

S. Cedar Cr.

Volga R.

Grannis Cr.

Guttenburg

Mississippi R.

Joy Springs Cr.

Ensign Hollow Cr.

Pecks Cr.

Richmond Springs Cr.

Mossy Glen Cr.

Grimes Hollow Cr.

Backbone State Park

Bear Cr.

Twin Bridge Cr.

Little Turkey R.

(52)

Fountain Springs Cr.

Bankston Cr.

Dubuque

Manchester

Manchester Fish Hatchery

Lower Swiss Valley Cr.

Upper Swiss Valley Cr.

Spring Branch Cr.

Maquoketa R.

(151)

(61)

IOWA

**Driftless Area
Stream Locator Map**
Northeast Iowa

CHAPTER 1
RESOURCES

Becoming acquainted with the Driftless Area spring creeks is a matter of using the appropriate resources. This book will be a good start. Two indispensable overviews for identifying and locating streams that hold trout are two series of maps: (1) the trout stream maps either provided by each state when you purchase a license and a trout stamp or at respective Department of Natural Resource offices (see References) and (2) the *DeLorme Atlas and Gazetteer* for Iowa, Minnesota and Wisconsin, readily available. "Trout Fishing Access in Southeastern Minnesota," an important booklet showing every area stream as well as all public and improved sections, is available from the Minnesota DNR (see References). Keep these publications in your car—within reach. You never know when you'll need them!

Two years ago on Montana's Bighorn River, I hired a guide originally from the Chatfield area of Minnesota. He not only showed me some fine black caddis action on the Bighorn but also drew some very valuable circles on page 26 of my *Minnesota Gazetteer*. One of the streams he noted produced one of the finest 'hopper fishing days I've experienced. My gazetteers are full of penciled circles of sections of streams with many notes in the margins, notes that say "large rainbows," "lots of beaver dams," "Look at this during the early season," "no," and so forth. With the gazetteer, I can tell a friend to fish Rush Creek (Crawford County, Wisconsin) "right below the power line," and he will know exactly where to go.

Some general observations may be made by viewing these maps. The trout streams usually become fly-fishable within 2 or 3 miles of their origin and will hold trout a few miles below the "designated trout water." If a stream flows into a larger river that is not "trout water," you can bet the larger river will also hold trout and may be worthy of exploration.

Other maps may prove valuable. County plat books, available at the county courthouse, provide maps showing every parcel of land and the name of the landowner of each parcel. These maps are useful for contacting landowners. Public lands, owned by the DNR and other government agencies, are also shown.

U.S.G.S. topographic maps are detailed and accurate. If you intend to learn every inch of a particular river, a "topo" map is important. Map services are listed in the Yellow Pages.

Also use the Internet to acquaint yourself with any trout stream. The Web site http://terraserver.com provides satellite image data for many streams of the area. After accessing the Web site, type in the name of the city nearest the stream (or enter the latitude/longitude), click "image data," and proceed. At the image size of 1 square meter/pixel, riffles and pools of larger streams are visible. Riffles on the lower reaches of the larger rivers are the best areas to find fish, and these riffles may be few and far between. Knowing where to find them can save much time when exploring for large trout.

Also available are several regional trout-fishing guide books, two of which deal with portions of the Driftless Area. John van Vliet's *Trout Fishing in Southeast Minnesota* provides maps and valuable commentary about finding and fishing 55 streams in southeast Minnesota. Jene Hughes's *Iowa Trout Streams* provides a guide to many northeast Iowa creeks. His book has led me down many gravel roads to explore streams new to me.

Portions of two other books include information about our spring-creek domain. In the first, *Exploring Wisconsin Trout Streams*, Steve Born, Jeff Mayers, Andy Morton and Bill Sonzogni include nine southwest Wisconsin streams, from the Kinnickinnick to the Mount Vernon, including stream management history, heritage, tactics, local information and more. One reviewer comments that this book makes her proud to be from Wisconsin.

The second book, *Wisconsin and Minnesota Trout Streams*, by Jim Humphrey and Bill Shogren, includes pertinent commentary about and fine maps of many rivers of southeast Minnesota and southwest Wisconsin.

An important publication of the Wisconsin DNR is "Wisconsin Trout Streams," a compendium of all state streams. Accurate maps and classification of stream quality are included.

The spring creeks of the Driftless Area are well covered in regional periodicals. *Midwest Fly Fishing*, published six times yearly, is available by subscription or at sporting goods outlets. It offers excellent local information by knowledgeable authors and was an important reference during the writing of this book. The Web site address is www.mwfly.com.

"Wisconsin Trout" and "Minnesota Trout," publications of the respective state Trout Unlimited organizations, are received by all members. Both are excellent. "The Flyline" is the newsletter of the Hawkeye Fly Fishing Association, an affiliate of the Federation of Fly Fishers, with membership information available at www.commonlink.com/hffa. Find complete information about all the previously mentioned publications in the Reference section.

The most reliable and current information, as usual, will come from the local fly fishers who are fishing daily. Many of them are in the highest level of the sport. In addition, both fly-fishing guides and owners of quality trout shops within and surrounding the region are readily available.

I hope that the resource material presented will be of value for your fly-fishing adventures in the Driftless Area.

As previously mentioned, the Driftless Area has year-round opportunities for fly fishing stream trout. Here is a month-by-month summary of the year 2000 regulations of each state, showing the various opportunities as they "open" or "close". Add future regulation changes in the spaces provided.

JANUARY AND FEBRUARY

Northeast Iowa: All streams are open.

Southeast Minnesota: The following streams are open, either in their entirety or in posted sections for catch and release (C & R), barbless hooks only:

Beaver Creek (tributary of main Whitewater River)
Camp Creek
Canfield Creek
Duschee Creek
East Beaver Creek (Beaver Creek Valley State Park)
Hay Creek
Main Branch Whitewater River
Middle Branch Whitewater River
South Branch Whitewater River
North Branch Whitewater River
North Branch Creek (Forestville State Park)
South Branch Root River

Southwest Wisconsin: All streams are closed.

_____

_____

_____

MARCH

Northeast Iowa: All streams are open.

Southeast Minnesota: The previously mentioned 12 streams remain open to C & R, barbless hooks.

Southwest Wisconsin: All streams open March 1 to C & R, artificial lures, barbless hooks.

_____

_____

_____

APRIL

Northeast Iowa: All streams are open.

Southeast Minnesota: All streams open April 1 to C & R, barbless hooks.

Southwest Wisconsin: Continues open to C & R, artificials only, barbless hooks.

_____

_____

_____

MID-APRIL

Northeast Iowa: All streams are open.

Southeast Minnesota: "Regular" season opens in mid-April. All streams are open; harvest is allowed, according to regulation.

Southwest Wisconsin: Remains open to C & R, artificials only, barbless hooks.

_____

_____

_____

MAY THROUGH MID-SEPTEMBER

Northeast Iowa: All are streams open.

Southeast Minnesota: Regular season remains open.

Southwest Wisconsin: Regular season opens May 1. All streams are open; harvest is allowed, according to regulation.

MID-SEPTEMBER THROUGH SEPTEMBER 30

Northeast Iowa: All streams are open.

Southeast Minnesota: All streams now C & R, barbless hooks.

Southwest Wisconsin: All streams are open.

OCTOBER, NOVEMBER, DECEMBER

Northeast Iowa: All streams are open.

Southeast Minnesota: All streams are closed.

Southwest Wisconsin: All streams are closed.

Checking the up-to-date regulations of each state is vital, of course, because changes occur annually. Even though "All streams are open," a portion of a stream—or an entire stream—may be closed for a special reason.

Iowa presents the only chance to fly fish in October, November and December. I have had incredibly good fishing during that time with excellent blue-wing olive and midge activity. Trout will take beetles and 'hoppers well into November. Be sure to wear a blaze-orange hat during the hunting season.

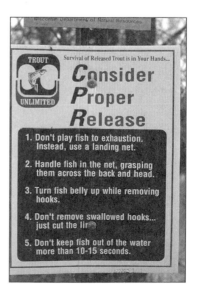

Wisconsin Department of Natural Resources

TROUT *Survival of Released Trout is in Your Hands...*

Consider Proper Release

UNLIMITED

1. Don't play fish to exhaustion. Instead, use a landing net.

2. Handle fish in the net, grasping them across the back and head.

3. Turn fish belly up while removing hooks.

4. Don't remove swallowed hooks... just cut the line.

5. Don't keep fish out of the water more than 10-15 seconds.

Chapter 1—Resources

Catch-and-Release Guidelines

Fly-fishing friend Clint Byrnes told me I had too little catch-and-release information in my first book. I agree. With the increase of special regulations requiring catch and release, these techniques should be clearly established. The best quote I have heard regarding catch and release came from Jim Bartelt of Madison, Wisconsin. While presenting a slide program to the Badger Fly Fishers, Jim said, "Imagine yourself running a 100-yard dash, and when you crossed the finish line, someone held your head under water for 20 seconds. Reversing the situation, this is exactly what is done to a landed trout." I think of these words often when handling trout.

- Play and land the trout efficiently.
- Use barbless hooks. A lip-hooked fish with a barbless hook need not be removed from the water. Simply remove the hook with your fingers or a hemostat.
- Wet your hands before handling a fish. Be gentle. Turn the fish upside down to remove the hook.
- Carry a net. A net is usually not needed for landing small trout. However, a net is often needed for large fish, especially in weedy areas or in situations in which the fish cannot be beached.
- Return the trout within 10 to 15 seconds. If you're having difficulty freeing the hook, give the fish a "breather" in the water; then try again. If the tippet/leader is wound around the gill area, unwind it immediately to allow the gills to move.
- Revive the trout in the water by pointing its head into the current. If there is little current, move the fish back and forth to allow water exchange through the gills.

Use of Stomach Pumps

The *Catch and Release Guidelines* booklet of the Federation of Fly Fishers does not recommend the use of stomach pumps because unless fishers are properly trained, the procedure may be fatal to the fish.

Experienced fly fishers have mixed opinions regarding pumping. Some feel that judiciously used—only one pump of fish of 12 or more inches—pumping may be used. On my home waters, I have not witnessed dead fish despite day-to-day fishing and pumping suitably sized fish.

Pumping is a good learning tool, revealing food objects taken by trout. However, it has limitations. Remember, the diet of a 12- or 14-inch fish may be far different from that of an 18-inch fish. Also, large food items, such as minnows and crayfish, do not show up in pumped samplings.

CHAPTER 2
EXPLORING

Exploring trout streams is the only way to learn for yourself the fly-fishing potential of a stream. Sometimes I must force myself to explore new water or review a stream I haven't fished for a few years. Exploring broadens you; it either adds to (usually) or subtracts from (sometimes) your repertoire of streams. Fly fishers lacking the exploring spirit have such a narrow range of choices that when the section of stream they like to fish is occupied, they have few alternatives. If you are the one occupying "their" stretch, you may have unwelcome company.

Exploring is an ongoing process because streams continually change. For example, changes can be caused by events such as storms. In June of 1998, a powerful storm with hurricane-force winds occurred in the La Crosse area. The flooding altered the streambed by either scouring or silt deposition. Microburst winds leveled large trees, many of which fell into the creeks. Fortunately, DNR crews cleared these trees on public water. Some private sections are still difficult to fish because of downed trees.

Also, pastures may be replaced by ungrazed meadows, habitat improvement projects may be completed, fishing regulation changes may yield more or larger trout. Even creeks that seem not to change may hold few trout one year and hold many of them the next, perhaps because of better reproductive success or the influx of new fish.

I view exploring with the fly rod as covering a lot of water, a bit different from my usual fishing sessions. Instead of meticulously dissecting every riffle or pool, I cast just often enough to satisfy myself about the presence of trout and then move on. (I do slow down if I hit a concentration of fish!) When exploring, I'm prepared to hike.

The early season is the best time to explore; gather your information in advance, and use it the rest of the season. March and April are especially good because you can avoid the heavy snow of winter and the vegetation of summer. Aquatic weed growth is minimal, allowing better evaluation of the streambed and easier probing with the fly. It can be surprising to return in August to a stream visited earlier and find it narrowed and deeply channeled by aquatic vegetation. Another advantage of March and April exploration is that the snow has flattened bankside vegetation. It's like walking on a sidewalk!

Also, at this time our spring creek trout begin to feed in earnest. As a result, chances of connecting with a large fish are excellent. Both Minnesota and Wisconsin have "delayed harvest" regulations that permit catch-and-release fishing early in the year and then allow harvest at a later date. My streamside notes include an entry of April 29, 1998: "Hooked 7 browns over 19 inches, 4 on Yellow Fox and 3 on scuds." These fish were caught and released on a lower stretch of a river located below "designated trout water." March and April are my best two months for large numbers of large trout.

On the other hand, there are disadvantages to exploring and fishing during these months. Expect at least a week or two of very cold or snowy weather early and heavy rain or wind later in the period (see Color Plate 4). These conditions are poor for our exploring and fishing efforts.

Choosing a stream to explore is easy; any stream will do. As mentioned previously, I favor checking the lower marginal reaches of trout water early in the year. Much of this land is private, and you will meet many landowners when asking for fishing permission. Be sure to let them know that you release all fish. Somewhat surprising to me is the number of landowners who are amazed that someone would release fish (even though required by law!). It is good to let these owners see a catch-and-release fly fisher standing right there in front of them!

Plan to explore on a sunny day with clear water. Wear polarized sunglasses and look closely for trout. If you are not moving or seeing fish, kick beneath undercut banks or logs to flush them. Trout may be absent for fairly long reaches of river; then one area may hold a pod of several fish. Learn to recognize the characteristics of water that holds trout, usually a riffle with a drop-off of good depth and often in the vicinity of a submerged log or a large bankside tree. Cobble bottoms with some larger stones are good—silted areas are bad. It is good to have a "feeding flat" nearby.

Be sure to make note of small cold feeders and wooded areas, especially those with riffles. Because these areas will be cool in mid- and late summer, large trout may congregate in them at that time, making the area worthy of a return visit.

Under proper lighting conditions, seeing into the deep pools is easy. You will almost certainly see fish. Don't let the large suckers, carp or red horse mislead you. Learn to recognize rough fish. The pectoral fins of suckers contrast sharply with the body. Trout have less pectoral-fin contrast. Suckers at times show a definite contrast of the pectoral fins; the leading edge is quite light and the trailing edge dark. If a fish has a forked tail, it is not a stream trout. Carp and red horse can give the golden-tone appearance of a large brown trout, but they have forked tails and move their tails with a looser "wiggle" or sway than trout. Brown trout have square tails that usually appear dark at the tip with a lighter band in front. A large brown may give the appearance of faint "stripe" over a cobbled stream bed. Also, trout have a faster "wiggle" when they swim. At times the white mouth of a brown trout will be visible. Mistaking a carp for a trout and fishing for it is okay (carp can be very tough). However, mistaking a trout for a carp and passing it by or startling it is not okay.

At the opposite end of the exploring spectrum are the upper reaches of streams. Some creeks that are just a trickle under the bridge may have some impressive pools higher up. Recently I hiked up a small Minnesota spring creek that in most cases could be stepped across. After about 30 minutes and three casts, however, I discovered an impressive pool full of trout, including one bona fide 20-inch brown. That fish proved to be uncatchable. Two small bobbers hanging from tree branches over the pool indicated to me that the fish had probably been well educated by locals—locals needing work on casting skills. This small stream also shares another characteristic with other streams worth exploring: It flows in a valley that has no road (see Diagram 2).

Tiny headwater streams, because they are so important to the health of the river downstream, have in many cases undergone habitat improvement by the Department of Natural Resources or other groups. Exploring the improved sections of these creeks can be a pleasant surprise. One very small tributary of the Little La Crosse River (Monroe County, Wisconsin) produced nine brown trout within the 45 minutes needed to cover the one improved section. Three of these

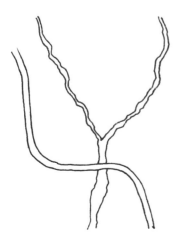

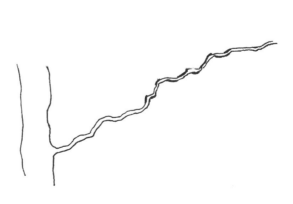

Diagram 2
Explore a stream that flows in a valley without a road.

Diagram 3
Explore the improved sections of small tributaries.

fish were between 15 and 16 inches. I found the stream by asking DNR person-nel. Signs stating "Public Fishing" were "absent" (see Diagram 3).

Be prepared to explore at even a hint of large trout. If a good fly fisher you know is "vague" or if you see his or her car parked in an unusual location, check it out. I know one fly fisher who parked his car at a wayside on a busy highway near the middle and lower reaches of a well-known creek. He then secretively removed himself to the upper sections of the creek where the large brook trout reside, unbeknownst to the fly anglers fishing the middle and lower reaches.

There are a number of flies I favor for early season exploring. At times, on large streams and rivers, I walk downstream casting a streamer that will usually reveal good numbers of trout if they are present. Streamers are excellent because they move trout in all kinds of water: riffles, runs or slow pools. Use a visible fly so that you can track it in the water. My current favorite exploring streamer is the Yellow Fox.

Yellow Fox

Hook: Daiichi® 2220, TMC® 5263—size 6, 10, 14

Thread: UNI-Thread®, black 6-0

Head: Black glass bead—size 8-0

Weight: None

Tail: Yellow marabou

Body: Kreinik® gold braid (#2000)

Underwing: Yellow marabou

Overwing: Fox squirrel tail

Tying Notes: This is a straightforward tie. Crimp the barb and add the glass bead. Start the thread and wind to the hook bend. Tie in the tail and the gold braid, advance the thread to the eye, wind the gold braid forward and tie off, allowing a bit of room behind the bead for the "wings." Tie in the underwing just short of tail length; then tie in the squirrel tail just longer than the tail. It is best to measure the squirrel tail and trim the butt end before tying in. Whip finish behind the bead; then cement.

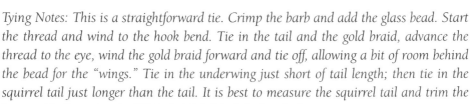

Fishing Notes:

The Yellow Fox is fished down and across with the hook size determined by stream size. Size 10 is my most-used hook. The Yellow Fox is probably at its best in long, slow runs. Cast the fly to within inches of the opposite bank, let it start to swing, feed out a bit of line and let the fly slowly continue the swing. Keep the rod tip straight with the fly line. Let the trout take the fly "on its own." There is little need for a hard strike, just a sideways flick of the rod tip. Sometimes a twitch of the rod tip immediately after the fly hits the water can trigger a strike. A slowly swinging Yellow Fox has produced multiple 20-inch brown trout for me (see Color Plate 6). In deep "powerful" water, add a Water Gremlin-brand® split shot at the hook eye; it is easily removed when you arrive at the next section of slow water. Look for underwater structure and bankside cover, and probe these areas with the fly.

When fishing streamers and similar flies, I usually use a shorter leader system (see later) and Maxima® tippet material in the 3- to 5-pound class.

When fishing downstream, avoid kicking up mud; cross at riffles. To stay out of the view of the trout, make longer casts.

For upstream exploring during the early season, Tom Wendelburg's All Marabou Leech, modified only with a glass bead at the eye, is an excellent choice.

Black Leech

Hook: Mustad® 9672—size 6, 10, 14

Thread: UNI-Thread ®, black 6-0

Head: Black glass bead—size 8-0

Weight: Heavy

Tail: Black marabou—Natural gray turkey marabou is also excellent.

Body: Black marabou

Tying Notes: Crimp the barb, add the glass bead and then add the weight. (For a size 10 hook, starting at midshank, wind .020 lead forward 12 turns; then double back for 4 turns. Use .025 lead for size 6, .015 for size 14.) Secure the lead with thread; then wind the thread to the hook bend. Tie in the tail; then use the thread to wrap, riblike, over the forward extension of the tail to create a thin abdomen. If needed, dub marabou on the thread to create an enlarged thorax. Tie off. Brush back the thorax and the abdomen with Velcro to give a shaggy appearance.

Fishing Notes:

The Black Leech can be moved as needed on the drift or retrieve without appearing unnatural. It has excellent action and is surprisingly visible. Despite being heavily weighted, it enters the water without excessive disturbance and gets deep quickly. A size 14 Black Leech paid unexpected dividends to me in mid-June on Mormon Coulee Creek in La Crosse County, Wisconsin. Dry-fly fishing with a caddis pattern had been fair, but I kept spooking trout from unpromising shallow areas. Closer inspection revealed hundreds of pollywogs in the shallows. The Black Leech proved to be a deadly imitation, even in deep water. Carrying a few unweighted patterns in June is a good idea.

For upstream exploring, I also favor scud patterns in orange and gray. Use a size 10 or 12 Orange Scud in discolored water and a size 16 Gray Scud in low, clear streams. Even midging trout will take a small "Neutral" Scud from the bottom in clear water. I have seen fish ignore my best efforts with a midge yet, on the first cast, take a small Gray Scud tied on 7x. Pattern descriptions for these flies appeared in my earlier book.

My friend Norm Zimmerman has extensive experience fishing coulee streams and favors scud patterns for early season exploring. Presented here are Norm's ties for the Orange Scud and the Tan Scud, which he prefers to the Gray Scud. During the early 1999 season, these flies accounted for 5 brown trout over 20 inches.

Tan Scud

Hook: TMC® 2457—size 12-18 (favors 14)

Thread: UNI-Thread®, orange or tan 6-0

Weight: .015 lead (10-12 turns on size 14)

"Antennae": Red squirrel tail fibers

Tail: Red squirrel tail and Krystal Flash®

Shell back: Plastic strip, Scud Back® or Mylar 3/16"

Rib: Copper wire, small

Body: Hare's Ear Plus®, tan. Can add Lite Bright® pearl-blue flash, chopped.

Orange Scud

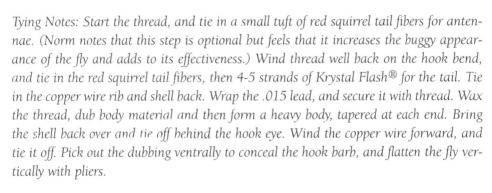

Hook: TMC® 2457—size 12-18 (favors 14)

Thread: UNI-Thread®, orange 6-0

Weight: .015 lead (10-12 turns on size 14)

Antennae: Red squirrel tail fibers

Tail: Red squirrel tail fibers and Krystal Flash®, orange

Shell back: Mylar strip

Rib: Copper wire, fine

Body: Rabbit, dyed orange with mixed, chopped Lite Brite® pearl-blue flash.

Tying Notes: Start the thread, and tie in a small tuft of red squirrel tail fibers for antennae. (Norm notes that this step is optional but feels that it increases the buggy appearance of the fly and adds to its effectiveness.) Wind thread well back on the hook bend, and tie in the red squirrel tail fibers, then 4-5 strands of Krystal Flash® for the tail. Tie in the copper wire rib and shell back. Wrap the .015 lead, and secure it with thread. Wax the thread, dub body material and then form a heavy body, tapered at each end. Bring the shell back over and tie off behind the hook eye. Wind the copper wire forward, and tie it off. Pick out the dubbing ventrally to conceal the hook barb, and flatten the fly vertically with pliers.

Fishing Notes:

Norm says that he uses the scud patterns routinely for early season fishing "because they match the stomach contents of the trout." Standard nymphing techniques—fishing upstream with an indicator—are used. He prefers a 9-foot, 4-weight rod with fast action.

In heavy or discolored water, use the Orange Scud in size 12 or 14 with added weight and 5x tippet. Norm likes to stay "in contact" with the fly by maintaining a fairly tight line. This technique allows for a quick strike at any indication of a take. Trout rapidly eject subsurface artificials. In clear water conditions, the Tan Scud in size 16 or 18 is used, most often with 6x tippet.

Scud imitations, of course, are not limited to early season exploring. They can be fished at any time. The "naturals" are especially numerous in aquatic vegetation. Norm says, "If you see watercress, think of scuds."

Scud patterns are Norm's favorite as the upper fly of a two-fly rig, which he often uses in clear water. The trailing fly is often a small Dark Nymph. It is noteworthy that small dark nymphs, size 18 and smaller, are often mentioned by expert fly fishers as very useful patterns. I favor the very simple One-Biot Nymph as a trailing pattern.

One-Biot Nymph

Hook: TMC® 921—size 20

Thread: Black 8-0

Weight: None

Tail: Black goose biot

Abdomen: Krystal Flash®, black

Thorax: Black Australian opossum

Wing case: Black goose biot

Tying Notes: Start the thread, and take it to just beyond the bend of the hook. Tie in the goose biot flat with just a short portion of the tip curving downward for the tail. Tie in the Krystal Flash®. Advance the thread, winding it over the biot, to the center of the shank. Stand up the biot at this point to be used later as a wing case. Advance the thread a few more wraps; then wind the Krystal Flash® forward to create a thin abdomen, and tie it off in front of the standing biot. Dub the Australian opossum, and create a pronounced thorax. Pull the biot over as a wing case, and secure it just behind the hook eye. Whip finish on the bare hook in front of the biot; then snip the thread and the biot.

Many streams, such as the South Branch of the Root River in Fillmore County, Minnesota, and the Rush River in Pierce County, Wisconsin, have good populations of black stone flies. A Bead Head Prince Nymph is a superior early season exploring pattern (see Color Plate 6). Also, note the Root River Special, a Wayne Bartz pattern discussed in the "Contributing Experts" chapter.

Bead Head Prince Nymph

Hook: TMC® 3761—size 10, 14

Thread: UNI-Thread®, black 6-0

Head: Brass bead, small

Weight: 9 wraps of .020 lead on size 10

Tail: Black goose biots (2)

Rib: Gold tinsel or wire

Body: Peacock herl, 3 strands

Wing: White biots (2)

Hackle: Brown soft hackle, 3 winds

Tying Notes: Crimp the barb; add the bead and the weight. Secure the lead with thread. Tie in the tails (see Diagram 4), ribbing and peacock herl. Reinforce the peacock by winding it around the tying thread, then advancing it. Wind the rib, and apply the wings in a "V" flat over the back. Tie in and wind the hackle. Tie off behind the bead.

Fishing Notes:

Use standard up-and-across nymphing techniques. Concentrate on the riffles. I generally use 5x tippet and a strike indicator. At times, added weight or a smaller trailing nymph is added.

Early season exploring with a dry fly can be surprisingly rewarding. My current favorite is the Brown Hackle Peacock Beetle (BHP Beetle). I am uncertain whether the trout take it for a dark stone fly or a beetle, but they do take it. Try it.

Diagram 4
Top view of hook. Tie in the biot tails on each side of the hook, flat sides vertical with the tips flaring outward.

Brown Hackle Peacock Beetle (BHP Beetle)

Hook: Daiichi® 1280, TMC® 100—size 12, 16

Thread: UNI-Thread®, black 8-0

Overbody: Black Hi-Vis®

Underbody: Peacock, 3 strands

Hackle: Brown saddle

Tying Notes: Start the thread; then tie in a medium "sheaf" of Hi-Vis®, starting one-third length behind the hook eye. Wrap Hi-Vis® to the rear of the hook just beyond the bend. (The backward protruding Hi-Vis® sheaf will be pulled over, wing case style, later.) Tie in the saddle hackle, then 3 strands of peacock. Advance the thread, advance the peacock and tie off a bit behind the eye. Wind the saddle forward 7-9 turns, and tie off. Trim the upwardly protruding hackle fibers; then pull over and tie down the Hi-Vis®, leaving a forward extension to mimic the head. With the thumb and forefinger, splay the downward protruding hackles to each side of the hook; then add a touch of cement to head.

Fishing Notes:

In early April, I have seen black beetles crawling across the snow! (See photograph, page 67.) At this time dry flies may become very effective exploring patterns. I have been very impressed with the size 12 BHP Beetle. Start with the beetle about mid- to late morning; use a 5X tippet, and stay with it. Trout willingly rise to this fly or at least take a look. Exploring with a large dry fly is an enjoyable way to fish. I appreciate especially the visual aspects and the casting. The BHP Beetle has replaced the Pass Lake as a favored exploring pattern except under conditions of poor visibility.

Although the BHP Beetle is primarily a daytime fly, I've had good results with a size 16 in the evening with fish rising to other hatches. There is no "wrong" way to fish this pattern; up- or downstream, with dead drift or action—all may be effective.

CHAPTER 3
EQUIPMENT

Rods

Fishing the coulee country with only one rod is like golfing 18 holes with only one club; and although I do know a few good fly fishers who confine themselves to only one rod, most use two or three rods for various fishing sessions.

Finding a rod suitable for the stream you fish most can be a pleasant task. First of all, fly-fishing shows with representatives from various rod companies, plus a casting pond, offer excellent opportunities to discover, test and compare new rods. Carry a notebook to record observations. Select one rod that may meet your requirements, cast with the rod and compare it with a second. Take the better of the two, and compare that one with a third, and so forth. Remember to check short-range performance and accuracy. Do not be intimidated by other casters double-hauling to 75 feet. After deciding which rod fits your needs, go to the local fly-fishing shop to retry it, again comparing it with one or two others. At this time, using your own reel and line is helpful.

Also take advantage of any information or opinions available from friends, guides and shop owners, but be sure to test the rod and make your own decision. I have made a couple of expensive mistakes by failing to try a rod after hearing an enthusiastic recommendation.

My current rod collection allows me to fish all kinds of streams in the coulee country, from the tiny upper reaches of the West Beaver Creek to the large pools of the main branch of the Whitewater. The stream I fish more often than any other is the medium-sized Timber Coulee special regulation section in Vernon County, Wisconsin. If rising trout are present during a fishing session, I usually approach to within 25 to 30 feet of them. Casting distance will be 26 to 32 feet if the fly is placed a foot or two above the fish. Usually these trout are taking small flies, size 18 and smaller, from the surface and film. If no risers are present, my next choice is either nymphing or fishing larger attractors. The larger flies, longer casting distance and possible addition of weight require more of a rod than the short casts with small dry flies.

I use a 3-weight rod of medium-to-fast action and at least 7 feet 9 inches in length for mending purposes and for keeping the line out of high weeds. This kind of rod is satisfactory in small headwater streams as well. However, on windless evenings, I often use a 2-weight rod.

For fishing large rivers with minnow imitations, leeches and large terrestrial patterns, I often use a 5-weight, $8^{1/2}$- to 9-foot rod with medium-to-fast action. An experienced fishing companion and I fished a large river in April during the Brachycentrus caddis hatch. He decided to use a 3-weight, 7-foot rod but discovered that this rod was inadequate in many respects: casting distance, mending, handling a breeze and casting large flies. We returned to the car and strung up a 4-weight, 9-foot rod that proved to be a great improvement.

For coulee area fly fishers, a 3- and a 5-weight rod in the lengths previously noted should manage most situations, with a 4 weight being the one-rod compromise.

It is interesting to compare the various opinions of anglers regarding fly rods. I know two expert fly fishers who prefer 2-weight rods for nearly all fishing and others who use 5 weights almost exclusively. My preference is to use a variety of rods to suit different conditions. Here is a list of my current most-used rods (all graphite):

Line Wt	Length	Action	Comments
2	8'2"	Medium	An excellent rod for small-to-medium streams. Good for small flies and difficult fish. Will handle small-weighted nymphs and leeches. Fun to fish. An 11-inch fish feels like a giant. Not for breezy conditions.
3	8'0"	Fast	Very accurate. Very good for terrestrial patterns, size 10 and smaller, on small, medium and even large streams. Will handle a breeze. Good for nymphing sighted fish and will handle some weight.
3	8'9"	Medium	The rod I favor for large, smooth pools and flats. Will delicately handle long casts with small flies. Good for swinging soft hackles.
4	8'6"	Medium-fast	An all-around rod except for very small water. Good in wind and handles a large spectrum of flies both unweighted and weighted. Credited with hundreds of fish.
5	8'6"	Fast	Large water, dirty water, streamers, leeches, 'hoppers, hexes, June bugs, wind, rain, extra weight, etc.

There is no reason not to use a 4- or 5-weight, 9-foot rod on our streams. Consider the extra length if you make trips to Western streams. Also, consider a 4- or 5-piece travel rod if you plan to fish distant destinations. Specialty rods— such as 0- and 1-weight rods, 7-foot 5-weights ('hoppers-in-the-brush) may suit some anglers. 6- or 7-weight, 9-foot rods may be of use on our largest rivers.

Reels

For our small natural creeks, I prefer a quiet reel, either no-click or "very quiet" click. Loud reels disturb wildlife. Judging by the reaction of small birds and animals nearby, a loud reel must sound like an alarm call. Other reel features are well known. A light-weight reel is not as tiring to use and does not interfere with rod balance as does a heavier reel; and a smooth easily adjusted drag system is important every time a large trout is being played. A large arbor reel is a good choice when "a lot of line is going out and a lot of line is coming in."

Fly Line

A dull gray or green fly line that does not frighten fish, floats well and shoots easily through the line guides is all that is needed for our streams. Clean the line frequently, especially when it has been used in dirty water. Lines that hold a coil do not shoot well and will therefore negatively affect the performance of the leader and the fly. If the line coils, try to stretch it before a fishing session. If the problem persists, purchase a more supple line.

To reduce the flash and visibility of a brightly colored line as it is cast over the trout, dye a 10-foot portion of the line to dull it. The process is easy (see Diagram 5).

Dyeing Fly Line

Use RIT® gray. To dissolve dye, follow package instructions. Set the boiling solution aside until it is hot, not scalding, to your finger. Place a 10-foot coil of line into the dye solution for about 10 seconds. (Do not dye the terminal two feet of line at the tip.) Remove the line and rinse it in cool water. This process usually significantly reduces the brightness of the line. If not, repeat the process, but avoid an unacceptably dark color. Caution: Use an old line for trials. Store any unused dye solution in a glass jar. For future use, reheat the mixture in a microwave. Most of my 2- through 5-weight lines are dyed, and neither their casting nor floating performance has been affected. However, I have not dyed "new generation" lines. At any rate, I am sure that dyeing a line voids the warranty.

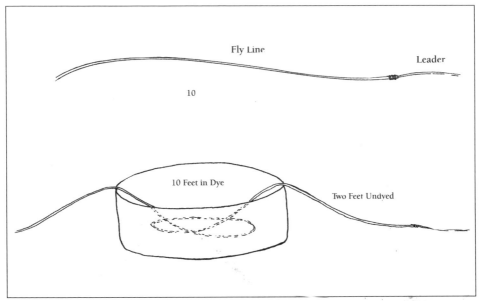

Diagram 5—Visibility is enhanced if the terminal two feet of fly line is undyed. There is no need to dye the entire line.

Leaders and Tippets

In the mid-1970s, my friend Dick Ward and I had reservations to fish Armstrong's Spring Creek near Livingston, Montana. Fortunately, we hired a guide, T. J. LaViolette. Without him, I doubt that we would have caught a fish. The first thing T. J. did on arriving in the parking lot was to strip about 40 feet of fly line from our rods. He then cleaned each line and inspected and rebuilt each leader. The process took about 20 minutes, and during that time several anglers entered the river, making Dick and me rather nervous. T. J. explained the process, but at the time I thought it was too unimportant to record in my notebook. By the end of the day, Dick and I had taken good numbers of large trout; other anglers had not done nearly as well. That day my spring creek fishing skills were greatly increased, especially fishing for sighted fish, using small flies and learning the importance of a properly constructed leader/tippet combination. Proper leader/tippet balance can be more important than the fly.

I prefer tying my own leaders. Once constructed, they are needle-nail knotted to the end of the fly line and will stay there for a couple of seasons. The main advantage to tying your own leaders is that you know exactly the material, diameter and length with which you are working. Experimentation with leader design is then easy.

My current leader preferences reflect the work of George Harvey, Lefty Kreh, Roger Hill and others (see References). Here are four essentials:

- One system for all fishing—I found the system of looping an entire "midge leader" or "nymph leader" to a loop at the end of the fly line to be cumbersome.

- Base section of stiff material, terminal section of softer material—Read the George Harvey *Fly Fisherman* magazine article "Leaders for Selective Trout." (see References). Stiff base sections are important for handling roll casts, wind, weight and heavy flies.

- Base section "permanent"—The base section is needle-nail knotted to the end of the fly line and remains for a couple of seasons. The base sections need to be tough, and the material must not absorb water. I use Maxima® material. Some other commercial knotless tapered leader materials are easily abraded and absorb water, resulting in a curled opaque appearance and diminished performance.

- An easy-to-understand system—A simple color-coded system allows me to know exactly the lengths and diameters with which I am working (see Diagram 6). I use Maxima Chameleon® (brown) for all base sections except .017, which is Maxima® clear. I then count up or down from the .017 to ascertain the diameter, length and material. At the junction of the base and terminal sections, I use Maxima® (brown) connected to the softer material (clear) of the same diameters; for example, .013 Maxima® (brown) to .013 (clear) of the softer material of choice (Umpqua, Orvis super strong, Scientific Angler, and so forth.) Using materials of the same diameter when joining stiff material to soft material prevents stiff material from cutting into the soft material and also prevents hinging of the cast.

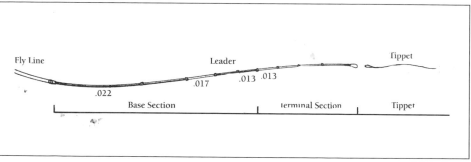

Diagram 6—Example of leader construction. The base section utilizes Maxima® material. The .017 segment is clear; all others are Chameleon (brown). The terminal segments are softer, clear materials of choice. Tippet segments may be looped or blood-knotted according to preference.

Leader Formula for 5- and 4-Weight Lines

Diameter	Length (inches)	Material	Color	Knot
.022	33	Maxima®	brown	
.020	22	Maxima®	brown	3-turn blood knot
.017	11	Maxima®	clear	3-turn blood knot
.015	5	Maxima®	brown	3-turn blood knot
.013	5	Maxima®	brown	3-turn blood knot
.013	5	softer material of choice	clear	4-turn blood knot
.011	8	material of choice	clear	4-turn blood knot
.009	10	material of choice	clear	4-turn blood knot-loop

Comment: Tie a loop (see Diagrams 7 & 8) at the end of the .009 system. To this loop is added whatever tippet is preferred. For example, if fishing streamers, simply loop a suitable length of 4x tippet. For dry flies, loop 4x; then add 5x or 6x with a blood knot, and so forth. Even 7x can be looped directly to the .009 loop. Leader/tippet length for fishing nymphs will be about two feet longer than the rod. Length for streamers will be shorter and for dry flies, longer. I like to have the .011 and .009 sections longer to allow retying new segments as the older ones are used. "Rebuilds" are necessary at times; being a few inches off here and there makes little difference. Some expert fly fishers feel that the loop-to-loop system increases the potential for drag. To avoid this problem, simply step down the leader with blood knots.

Leader Formula for 3- and 2-Weight Lines

Diameter	Length (inches)
.020	33
.017	22
.015	11
.013	5
.013	5
.011	5
.009	8
.007	10

Comment: The materials and colors match those of the 5- and 4-weight formula. For shorter rods, shorten the first three segments to 30, 20 and 10 inches. For softer rods, start with .017 clear Maxima® as the butt section and step down to a .010/.010 junction of the stiff/soft materials.

COLOR PLATE 1

Yellow Fox
p. 26

Orange Scud
(Tied by Norm Zimmerman)
p. 29

Bead Head Prince
p. 31

Black Leech
p. 27

Egg Fly
p. 52

One-Biot Nymph
p. 30

Fuzzball
p. 56

Hare's-Foot Light Cahill
p. 57

Brown Hackle Peacock
Beetle
p. 32

Black Sculpin
p. 53

COLOR PLATE 2

"One cannot spend a day astream without seeing or hearing many springs and feeders."

The temperature of this small feeder of the West Fork of the Kickapoo was 49° F. The stream temperature was 67° in mid-afternoon in late June.

"Conditions for the reproductive success of brown and brook trout, which spawn in fall, are favorable in many streams with good supplies of gravel for redds and oxygen-rich, silt-free groundwater sources for egg and fry development."

"If you follow an electrofishing stream survey crew, you will be amazed by the truly great numbers of trout present in many of our streams."

A tub of trout sampled from a bank run.

"Whether standing on a ridge top looking down or in a valley looking up, you will be impressed by the natural wooded bluffs with outcrops of bedrock."

COLOR PLATE 4

"Sometimes the walk back to the car after a session on the river is as enjoyable as the fishing itself." Near Billings Creek (Vernon County, Wisconsin).

"On the other hand, there are disadvantages to exploring and fishing in March and April. Expect at least a week or two of cold or snowy weather early, and heavy rain later in the period."

John Shillinglaw on Timber Coulee in March.

Diagram 7—Forming Loop in monofilament. See References—Fly Fishing the South Platte River *by Roger Hill.*

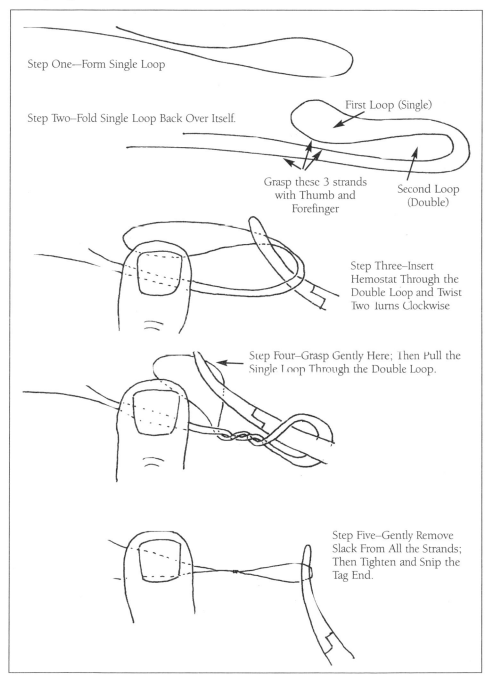

Step One—Form Single Loop

Step Two–Fold Single Loop Back Over Itself.

First Loop (Single)

Grasp these 3 strands with Thumb and Forefinger

Second Loop (Double)

Step Three–Insert Hemostat Through the Double Loop and Twist Two Turns Clockwise

Step Four–Grasp Gently Here; Then Pull the Single Loop Through the Double Loop.

Step Five–Gently Remove Slack From All the Strands; Then Tighten and Snip the Tag End.

I use the following "3-2-1" system to remember lengths of the first three segments of the base section:

"3-2-1" system

Long Rods	Short Rods
33"-22"-11"	30"-20"-10"

Construction methods are simple. Lay a yardstick on a bench, and line up the leader spools in order. Measure and cut the butt, allowing about 10 inches extra for the needle-nail knot line connection and the blood knot. Cut the next section, allowing an extra 1¹/₂ inches per blood knot. Work down the leader. Trim all tag ends at the knot, and with a toothpick, add a bit of Zap-A-Gap® to the first 6 or 7 knots. I have had only minor problems with moss or algae clinging to the knots. In the final few feet of leader, don't knot together sections that are more than a 2x difference in diameter. Seven and 8x are best knotted to the next "x" size (7x to 6x, 8x to 7x). Seven and 8x may be looped to larger x sizes, however. I use 5-turn blood knots with fine tippet material.

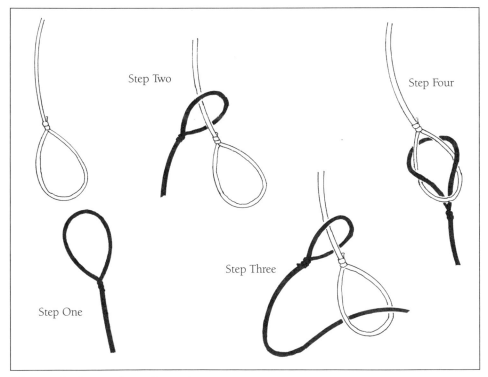

Step Two

Step Four

Step Three

Step One

Diagram 8—Loop-to-Loop Connection

Leader Construction Kit Components
Leader spools, folding yardstick, nippers, hemostat (for loop knot), Zap-A-Gap® and toothpicks.

Needle-Nail Knot Components
Sewing needles, a $1^1/2$ inch swizzle stick straw (the nail or tube), single-edge razor and small flat-head pliers. Instructions for tying the Needle-Nail Knot are given in *Practical Fishing Knots II* (see References).

During a day on the stream, many situations require leader/tippet adjustment; you will pay for laziness if these adjustments are not made. Keep leader materials easily accessible. Most leader problems have commonsense solutions. Here are a few examples:
• Before stringing your rod, strip some line from the reel. The leader will be coiled. To straighten the leader, hold it firmly between the thumb and forefinger and pull the line twice with the other hand, holding tightly enough to create some friction and heat. The leader should then be straight.
• When arriving at the stream, select the appropriate fly and tippet. Unless you know that the tippet presently on the leader is good, remove it and add a new tippet/fly combination. You are then ready to fish.
The following leader/tippet problems require correction:
• Wind knot(s) in the tippet.
• Tippet roughened and frayed from rocks or fish teeth. It is a good idea to tie on a new tippet after catching a few large fish.
• Curled or kinked tippet when fishing on top. The kinks are the result of overstretching, usually after catching a branch on the backcast or pulling too hard when tightening the knot while tying the fly to the tippet. This problem occurs most frequently with a 6x and 7x tippet. To prevent kinking while tying a small fly to a fine tippet, use a 4-turn improved clinch knot, moisten the knot and tighten it by gently pulling the far end of the tippet (away from the fly) with one hand and the fly with the other hand. (You can even pull on the tag end by biting with your teeth.) Tippet material that coils easily is an annoyance. To find suitable material, experiment with several brands.
• Waterlogged tippet. Most tippet material slowly absorbs water, developing an opaque grayish look. The tippet becomes very limp and adherent, making knots difficult to tie. Some materials are resistant to absorbing water, especially the fluorocarbons and Maxima®.
• Poor balance between leader and fly. In January 1992, I listened to Lefty

Chapter 3–Equipment

Diagram 9

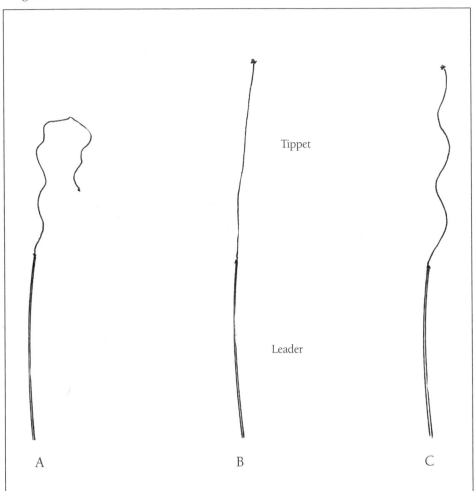

Tippet

Leader

A   B   C

Tippet Adjustments:

In Figure A, the tippet is either too long or too light for the fly being used. Accuracy will decrease. Either shorten the tippet or use heavier material.

In Figure B, the tippet is either too short or too heavy for the fly being used. Accuracy is excellent, but drag will be a problem. Either lengthen or lighten the tippet.

In Figure C, a proper balance of leader, tippet and fly is illustrated.

—From *Practical Fishing Knots II*, by Mark Sosin and Lefty Kreh,
Lyons and Burford Publishers, NY, NY 1991.

—Diagram used with permission of Lefty Kreh.

Kreh during a presentation sponsored by Wisconsin's Southern Chapter of Trout Unlimited. What he said was beautiful in its simplicity. This information is available in *Practical Fishing Knots II*, by Mark Sosin and Lefty Kreh (see References and Diagram 9), and has appeared in other publications.

On the stream, I carry the following materials: spools of standard leader material from 2x to 7x (occasionally 8x) in a convenient dispenser; for its stiffness and toughness, two spools of Maxima® in the 2- to 5-pound class; and two spools of fluorocarbon in 7x and 5x for difficult fish on small flies or terrestrials. In addition, in the back pocket of my vest I carry two pre-tied leaders for those rare ugly situations that require cutting the entire leader plus the tip of the fly line and tying on a complete new leader.

Wading Gear

My first choice of wading gear for coulee country streams is waist-high Gore-Tex® stocking-foot waders combined with wading boots having "sticky" rubber soles. The waist height rarely limits stream crossing yet allows one to sit on the bank (even in the stream on hot days) without getting a wet butt as with hip boots. I often sit to watch the stream or to fish, examine insect specimens and untangle tippets. I also appreciate not having the weight of suspenders on my shoulders. I have yet to talk with an angler who does not prefer breathable waders. For cold conditions, just add insulation; for rainy conditions, be sure your rain jacket is long enough. However, sometimes chest-high waders are best. An all-day rain or deep stream channels in watercress require these chest-high waders.

The sticky rubber-soled wading shoes are superior to felt-soled shoes on wet, grassy banks and in snow, but felt soles are better on wet rocks. Avoid the rubber soles, though, if you are fishing in the West from a guide's drift boat because these soles may leave scuff marks on the bottom of the boat.

I routinely wear kneepads cut from the calf/thigh area of worn-out neoprene waders. Kneepads are frequently needed in the coulee country.

Wet wading is fine on hot summer days.

CHAPTER 4
CASTING

Beginning fly casters should receive instruction immediately, before bad habits form. For experienced casters, one session with an instructor may result in lasting improvement, as I discovered after a session with Lou Jirikowic of Sheboygan, Wisconsin. My streamside notes contain ideas and techniques that have proved useful on our spring creeks:

• Practice casting in nonfishing situations. Develop a practice regimen, and work on areas of weakness. Short sessions are best. If possible, practice over water instead of grass so that you can work on keeping line spray away from the target area. Make loop control and accuracy part of every practice session. To improve casting accuracy, read Art Lee's *Fly Fisherman* magazine article "The Right Foot Forward," (see References).

• Learn a variety of casts. The *straight-line cast* is, of course, essential. Remember that where and how the fly line lands are as important as where and how the fly lands. Other frequently used casts include the following:

• *The check, or tuck, cast*—Steve Hilbers of the Bighorn Trout Shop in Fort Smith, Montana, says, "The difference between a good nympher and a great nympher is the ability to use this cast." Form the loop high on the forward cast with the rod held vertically and stop (check) the rod high to allow the nymph to swing under the stopped line (tuck) so that the nymph enters the water with the leader in the vertical position. This technique permits the fly to sink quickly with little weight.

• *The roll cast*—This cast is necessary in the absence of space for the back-cast, a common situation. Remember to stop the rod tip high rather than driving it toward the water.

• *The reach cast*—The reach cast is used routinely to allow a longer drag-free drift, especially when fishing across or down to a trout.

• *Positive and negative curve casts*—I routinely use negative curve casts when casting searching-type dry flies (terrestrials, attractors, elk hair caddis, and so forth) upstream (see Diagram 10). With the rod canted horizontally, cast an underpowered loop so that the fly lands near the bank before the loop straightens. This technique places the tippet farther from the trout and allows a longer drag-free float than a straight-line cast does. A fly fisher casting with either hand will use the left hand to execute this cast to the left bank and the right hand to cast to the right bank. Occasionally, I use positive curve casts to place the fly around the inside bend of an upcoming corner in the stream.

• *The downstream cast—* When fishing directly down to a fish, aerialize more line than is necessary to reach the fish. When the line has straightened on the forward cast, pull the fly back toward you; then let it fall to the water and drift to the fish. Casting down and across is a more common situation and usually requires an upstream reach cast.

• Learn to cast with each hand. This skill is mastered with difficulty, but once the skill is accomplished, you will use and benefit from it in countless fishing situations. Begin practicing on a large stream with few casting obstacles. Force yourself to use the nondominant hand, and stay with it. This time is well spent. Being "ambicastrous" helps every time you fish around a bend in the river and whenever a backcast obstacle is present, very common situations on coulee streams. Also, whenever the wind blows, use the downwind hand. When casting down and across to a trout, use the upstream hand, thereby keeping the fly line out of view of the fish. Then extend the drift by passing the rod to the downstream hand.

• Learn the *double-haul*. Mel Krieger's video "The Essence of Fly Casting" makes learning the double-haul easy.

• Store stripped-in line in loops on your line hand. Otherwise, when you retrieve line, it may fall at your feet, become tangled in vegetation, be dirtied in the mud or be pulled downstream by the current, thereby hindering the next

Diagram 10
Negative curve cast.

Current

cast. Gathering the retrieved line in your line hand increases casting success. Read the E. Neale Streeks *Fly Fisherman* magazine article "Line Control: putting stripped line in its place" (see References).

• Learn to cast weighted flies and two-fly rigs. Be sure to have no slack line when you pick up for the backcast. Cast a wide loop, and minimize false casting. Wait for the backcast to straighten (with weight, you'll feel a "clunk") before beginning the forward cast.

• False cast so that no line spray or flash occurs over the target. Do not cast the fly too far upstream from a rising or sighted fish because as it lands, the heavy portion of the leader may startle the trout.

CHAPTER 5
LARGE FISH

Large brown trout are survivors. One in a thousand yearling brown trout lives to be 16 inches. A stream-grown 20-inch brown is at least seven years old (see Color Plate 7). These fish have tremendous survival instincts and luck. In his writings, Tom Wendelburg describes their "caginess" and "warrior nature." I have referred to huge trout as "a different species" in my earlier book.

Not all large coulee trout are stream-raised, however. Some hatchery brood-stock fish are planted. Most rapidly disappear from streams that have no protective regulations; some survive and become increasingly difficult to catch.

The Driftless Area spring creeks, with their favorable conditions for trout growth, hold surprising numbers of browns in the 20-inch class. A proficient fly angler pursuing large fish should hook several each year. April and August are my best months for large browns, April because these fish are becoming very active and August because of terrestrial insect activity.

Large browns have food and shelter requirements different from those of their smaller kin. For shelter, large, deep pools, overhead cover, instream logs, rocks and shade are important. The presence of flat, shallow feeding areas is also important. These fish roam the flats and need space to roam at night. During the winter large fish require deep pools with low water velocity.

They become meat eaters; a forage base of fish, crayfish, leeches, even small mammals, is needed. These fish, however, do eat small food items and will feed at the surface.

Large browns also display some predictable behaviors: they respond to alarming stimuli, intently observe food in their vicinity, move upstream to spawning gravels in the fall, and so forth. Even "odd" behavior, if analyzed, makes sense. Trout behavior determines the methods we use to locate these fish.

A Western radio telemetry study of large brown trout behavior revealed that they held in shaded, sheltered areas during the day, then roamed over large distances in the darkness with peak activity at dusk and dawn. An exception was mid-summer, when trout movement corresponded to availability of terrestrial insects.

In some large coulee area streams, behavior of large trout differs from that expected. Finding large brown trout visibly feeding in shallow water during the daytime, either holding position in more rapid currents or patrolling the quiet, flat areas, is not uncommon. Because they are heavily fished, these trout become difficult, capable of detecting any error of approach or presentation.

Finding large trout requires a "large-trout mentality," a mind-set concerned with seeking these fish at every opportunity. Large fish are found by looking for them, and although they may be found anywhere, certain waters are more likely to hold them:

- The large lower reaches of streams, especially before harvest is allowed.

- Less frequently fished water. Ask fishing permission at farms located midway between widely spaced bridges.

- Catch-and-release streams.

- Tributary branches of large rivers in the fall.

- Streams that are difficult to fish.

However, methods of locating trout are not limited to knowledge of trout food and shelter requirements, behaviors and habitat preferences. For instance, I have located large brown trout by having them follow a smaller hooked fish that I was playing. Also, following an electrofishing stream survey crew is educational. I have located good trout with this "method." Read stream-stocking reports and stocking reports of brood-stock fish, especially if you are interested in photographs. In addition, talk with friends who spend long hours on the water. They often share the location of a large fish. Trout bums, if you can get them to talk, generally know the locations of many large fish. Trout bums, however, are difficult to contact. They are usually unemployed; therefore you cannot contact them at work. Calling them at "home" is similarly difficult because of their transient stays at various addresses, and sometimes "home" is a vehicle.

Many large "nonfeeding" browns are caught because they are vulnerable to the incidental food morsel (your fly) that happens to drift near them. Because

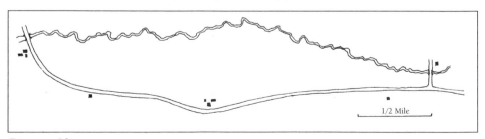

1/2 Mile

Diagram 10
Ask permission to fish at a farm halfway between two widely spaced bridges.

these fish are resting in protective sheltering lies, they have been unseen by the angler. Standard nymphing, dry-fly and streamer techniques (combined with a proper approach) allow the fly to enter the zone of the trout and to be taken. The angler is fishing to an "area" rather than to a trout that has been seen. Well-known areas with potential for holding large fish are log jams, habitat improvement structures and deep bank runs and pools, especially those with overhead cover.

Fishing to trout that have been seen is different from fishing to areas. When fishing sighted fish, begin the planning process as soon as the fish is seen because every move you make is meaningful. The process of stalking, looking and then finding the fish is of great importance. Remember that a sighted fish is closer and deeper than it appears.

A large sighted fish in shallow water demands the best fly-fishing skills. As noted previously, these fish are capable of detecting any error of approach or presentation. For instance, most will not tolerate a leader/tippet landing over them. They need to see the fly before seeing the tippet. Therefore, cast from above or from the side of the fish, and use fine tippets; for if the water is clear enough to see the trout, it is clear enough for the fish to see the tippet.

For a large trout feeding at the surface in shallow water, fish upstream and across from the fish. Use a low cast. Place the fly upstream and to the far side of the fish, mending the fly into the feeding lane; then let the fly drift over the fish. If the fish takes, strike with a short sideways flick of the rod tip. If the imitation is ignored, let it swing down and off to the side, retrieve and cast it again. The first cast is the most important. Flush-floating patterns, such as floating nymphs, emergers, parachutes or spinners, usually work best. Specific patterns will be discussed later.

Shallow-water trout feeding beneath the surface present a more difficult problem. Judgments about fly weight, current speed and drag potential need to be made. Because the fly cannot be seen easily, strike detection may be difficult. Watch the fish, and tighten at any hint of a take. Strike indicators are important; I use orange strike putty rolled over the blood knots of the leader. Use just enough to allow visibility, and place one or two indicators about an arm's length above the fly. Small scud, nymph and larva patterns tied with varying amounts of weight are usually used. If possible, avoid adding lead to the tippet because lead increases the potential for tangles and adds to the surface disturbance when the fly hits the water. Taking a large fish from shallow water with a small fly is a very satisfying experience.

Sighted fish in deep pools present different challenges. These fish, because of the depth, feel more secure and may continue to feed, even though they are aware of your presence (see Color Plate 7). Two techniques are useful. Try a heavily weighted size 6 Black Leech. Cast it upstream, and allow it to settle on the streambed near the fish. This pattern is very visible in the depths. Occasionally the trout will pounce on it. Often, however, the fish show an initial mild interest and then continue feeding on other items.

A second technique, the "deep-water egg indicator," is a bit more complicated. It combines an Egg Fly indicator with the previously mentioned One-Biot Nymph. (see page 30.) This technique is very effective.

Egg Fly

Hook: TMC 2457—size 16

Thread: UNI-Thread®, light yellow 8-0

Weight: None

Body: Egg Yarn®—Color: Oregon cheese

Tying Notes: Start the tying thread. Cut a one-inch section of Egg Yarn®, and tease it apart into four equal sections. With two loose turns of thread, attach one section to the top center of the hook. Then rotate this section to the bottom of the hook, and secure it with another wrap. Repeat with one more yarn section. (Keep all thread wraps on top of one another.) Attach the two remaining sections separately and securely to the top of the hook; advance the thread to hook eye without further binding of the yarn sections. Grasp and gather all yarn strands from the top and bottom, pull them upward and snip the entire bundle close to the hook shank. Primp the yarn to a spherical shape. The egg diameter should be about 3/16 inch.

Fishing Notes:

For fish visible in the deep, slow pools, use a long leader, and tie the Egg Fly to a length of 6x tippet; add a section of 7x to the hook bend, and tie on the One-Biot Nymph as a trailing fly. Cast the two-fly rig well upstream of the fish, and watch the Egg Fly indicator descend as the currents carry it toward the fish. On the first drift the fly will often pass a foot or two higher than the target. Recast farther upstream to allow the Egg Fly to pass at the level of the nose of the trout. Watch the fish. The take is indicated by any hint of movement. I have tightened at the wiggle of the tail and have been fast to very large fish. Occasionally the trout make the catch easy by eating the Egg Fly. My March 17, 1997, notes state,

"Took a brown trout over 20 inches on the Yellow Egg fly." This fish had been seen feeding in a deep pool. At times a microshot is needed; be careful not to add too much weight because it impedes the natural drift of the fly.

Large trout tend to be less cautious in heavy feeding situations initiated by terrestrial activity, concentrations of minnows, hatches of large insects, and so forth. Exploit these situations.

Certain climatic and light conditions seem to activate large browns. For example, fish become active in the period preceding a snowfall or a rainfall. They also become active in periods following a rainfall because rising stream levels increase the flow of food items. In addition, rainfall frequently produces muddy water, a prime condition for trout attacks on large vibration-causing prey items. A heavy sculpin imitation, which causes a disturbance in the muddy water, may produce a surprising result.

Black Sculpin

Hook: Mustad® 3399—size 2

Thread: Black 6-0

Head: Black Sculpin® wool

Weight/Eye: Dazl-Eyes ^{5}/32 nickel-plated lead

Tail: Black marabou

Abdomen: Black marabou, dubbed

Pectoral fins: Gray turkey wing coverts, large

Tying Notes: Tie in lead eyes about ^{1}/5-shank length behind the hook eye on top of the hook, Clouser style. Reinforce the tie-down area with Zap-A-Gap®. Run the thread to the hook bend, and tie in a thick tail. Dub the marabou to the thread, and create a thick abdomen, ending behind the eyes. Strip the base fibers from the quill of a large turkey wing covert feather, leaving enough fibers beyond the base to mimic the pectoral fin of a sculpin. Coat lightly with head cement. Tie one feather on each side, immediately behind the eyes. These feathers should protrude laterally from the fly and be cupped forward. Dub the Sculpin® wool on the thread, and form a large head, also taking two wraps behind the fins and crisscrossing between the eyes. Whip finish at the hook eye.

Chapter 5–Large Fish

Fishing Notes:

There is no need to use a fine tippet in muddy water; 3x is fine. The Black Sculpin hits the water with a noticeable plop, and the stiffly protruding pectoral fins create vibrations in the water as the fly is stripped in. This is an upside-down fly, resulting in few bottom snags. Retrieve the fly with short strips, which lift the fly from the stream bed. Then allow it to settle; then repeat.

Muddy conditions illustrate the importance of being familiar with "home waters." Despite being unable to see structure and snags beneath the surface, you will know their location. You will also know the location of the large fish.

Large trout favor low light conditions. Morning and evening shadows, dense cloud cover and darkness are well-known times to hook these fish. During daylight, fish the shady side of weed beds, banks, overhead structures, and so forth.

Large browns sometimes respond sharply to "something they can't have"; a minnow imitation falling within inches of a bank, or even bouncing off the bank, and then being rapidly stripped toward the angler may trigger an otherwise lethargic brown.

Fly anglers live for the take of a large fish. Once the fish is hooked, the excitement begins. The first impulse of the trout is to head for cover, and the fish knows exactly where that is. So should you. Immediately point the rod tip away from the direction you want the trout to run, hoping this technique will cause a change in the trout's path. If you can hop in the water and further discourage the fish from heading to shelter, do so. If at all possible, let the fish have its run. Do not snub the run of a freshly hooked fish. Get the fish on the reel as soon as possible. Either you or the fish should be gaining line. Lift the rod tip; then reel as you lower the tip, just like saltwater and steelhead fishing. When you reel, do so smoothly. Avoid pumping the rod up and down with each turn of the reel handle. Look for potential hazards; avoid them with side pressure on the fish.

A dangerous time is near the end of the fight; a suddenly panicked fish has often been lost at this point. Look for a place to beach the fish. If you are on the bank and can back up while beaching the fish, do so. If you are in the water, move the fish between you and the bank, but keep your legs together so that the fish cannot bolt between them! If the stream bed is muddy, stir up some mud in the water so that the fish doesn't see clearly. Put your hand beneath the fish, and beach it. In weedy areas or in situations in which the fish cannot be beached, use a net. Also, use a net to store the fish underwater while you get ready to photograph it. Remember the 100-yard dash analogy.

COLOR PLATE 5

Black Stone Fly Nymph
p. 61

Black Stone Fly Adult
p. 62

Tan Midge Larva
p. 63

Vinyl Rib Larva
p. 64

Olive Biot
Bow-Tie Pupa
p. 64

Dark Midge
Pupa
p. 65

Loop Wing Emerger
(Tied by Dick Ward)
p. 66

CDC Downwing
Midge Adult
p. 65

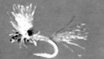

Midge Cripple
p. 66

Pheasant Tail
Nymph
(Weighted
Variant)
p. 71

Two-Biot
Nymph
p. 73

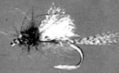

Shillinglaw Emerger
(Tied by John Shillinglaw)
p. 74

Parachute
Blue-Wing Olive
(Black Post)
p. 74

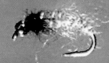

Olive Larva
p. 76

Brachycentrus
Pupa
p. 76

Brachycentrus
Adult
p. 77

"A slowly swinging Yellow Fox has produced multiple 20-inch trout for me."

A 21-inch brown with the Yellow Fox on the gill cover.

"Many streams, such as the South Branch of the Root River in Fillmore County, Minnesota, and the Rush River in Pierce County, Wisconsin, have good populations of black stone flies. A Bead Head Prince Nymph is a superior early season exploring pattern."

"Large brown trout are 'survivors.' One in a thousand yearling brown trout lives to be 16 inches. A 20-inch stream-grown brown is at least seven years old."

This fish took a minnow imitation from "marginal" trout water.

"Sighted fish in deep pools present different challenges. These fish, because of the depth, feel more secure and may continue to feed, even though they are aware of your presence."

This 25-inch brown, taken from a catch-and-release stream, pounced on a leech imitation.

"True to their name, Stone Fly Nymphs favor the rocky, riffled stream sections."

Norm Zimmerman lands a brown trout that took a Bead Head Prince Nymph in classic stone fly water. The high temperature of the day was 25°.

Rush River (Pierce County, Wisconsin).

Leech patterns are fished in the deep, slow pools during winter. *"Retrieving the leech should be 'painfully slow.' Most of the time the imitation should be resting on the bottom with only brief movements imparted by the retrieve. I watched Tom Wendelburg hook and land a 22-inch brown trout using exactly this technique in early February."* This is the fish.

CHAPTER 6
TWO-FLY SYSTEMS

E. Neale Streeks—fly angler, author and guide on Montana's Missouri River for over 20 years—introduced me to fishing two-fly systems. Neale used a size 18 Parachute Adams, which was threaded onto the section of leader above the tippet. Eighteen inches of tippet was then tied to this leader with a double surgeon's knot. This knot prevented the Parachute Adams from sliding onto the tippet. An unweighted size 20 dark nymph was then tied to the tippet. Stomach contents of our targeted "rising" trout had been found to be about 95% small dark nymphs and 5% Baetis duns. Our nymph imitation drifted just below the film with the naturals, and the Parachute Adams indicated many takes.

Two-fly systems are versatile and effective on our Driftless Area spring creeks. I now tie the tippet of the trailing fly to the hook bend of the lead fly on all my two-fly rigs. Here are some examples of common two-fly systems:

Dry Fly/Dry or Film Fly

In situations when the lighting makes tracking a small dry fly difficult, I use a white post parachute pattern teamed with a black post parachute. The white post is visible against dark backgrounds, and the dark post is easily seen with a light background. Film flies, such as small spinners, floating nymphs and midge pupae, are difficult to see. Simply add an indicator dry.

Dry Fly/Subsurface Fly

A small (size 18 or 20) visible and buoyant dry fly that will support a similarly sized nymph one or two feet beneath the surface is very important. The Fuzzball excels in visibility and buoyancy. It is also an excellent fly to fish singly. Indicator dry fly patterns may need to be changed occasionally if you are fishing from a stationary position because the trout may "get on" to them.

Fuzzball

Hook: TMC® 921—size 18, 20

Thread: UNI-Thread®, rusty dun 8-0

Tail: Wood duck flank feather fibers

Abdomen: Beaver, gray-olive

Wing: Snowshoe hare's-foot fibers

Thorax: Same as abdomen

Tying Notes: Crimp the barb, start the thread and tie in a short tail. Touch the thread wraps on the hook shank with a bit of silicone paste (tip of toothpick) to aid flotation. Dub the beaver, and wind a thin abdomen, ending one-third shank length behind the hook eye. Pinch a midsized bunch of snowshoe hare's-foot fibers, and snip it at the base. Remove the underfur without releasing the "pinch," and hold the hare's-foot fibers above the hook shank in a slanted back-wing position. Trim the butt fibers just behind the hook eye; then tie in wing firmly. The trailing wing fibers will extend beyond the tail. Add thorax dubbing, and create a noticeably thick thorax, taking several winds just behind the wing. Advance the thread and dubbing to the hook eye; then whip finish. Pinch the wing tips, push them forward a bit and snip so that the wing length extends just past the base of the tail.

Fishing Notes:

The Fuzzball is my most valuable small indicator dry fly. As previously mentioned, it will support a small nymph drifting beneath it. The combination of a size 18 Fuzzball and a size 18 Olive Nymph (ribbed with copper wire to allow sinking) was responsible for two brown trout, one over 19 inches and the other over 20 inches, on Poindexter's Slough near Dillon, Montana. Both fish were seen feeding in the flats, their white mouths visible when opening to take size 18 PMD nymphs in shallow water. From my position across and slightly above the fish, I cast several feet upstream from the trout to allow the nymph to sink to their level. Tippets were 7x to the Fuzzball and 7x to the nymph. Each take was registered by a sideways movement of the trout and a dip of the Fuzzball. Both fish were hooked in the center of the upper lip.

Hare's-foot-type dry flies were originally tied and described by Francis

Betters. Known as the Phillips Usual, these flies were modified and improved, notably by Art Lee (see References). The hare's-foot fibers have excellent floating characteristics: The "crisply crinkled" fibers create countless small air spaces and contain natural oils. The air spaces and oils also contribute to a decidedly translucent appearance on the water.

Hare's-foot-type dry flies may be tied as size 12 to 16 and used with larger nymphs, even bead heads. One of the best large indicator dry flies is the Hare's-Foot Light Cahill. This pattern is also excellent, used alone, on summer evenings when large yellow insects, such as light cahills, large sulphurs, crane flies and yellow stone flies, are on the water. The visible, durable pattern floats well.

Hare's-Foot Light Cahill

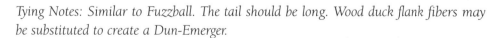

Hook: TMC® 100—size 12, 14

Thread: UNI-Thread®, light yellow 8-0

Tail: Bleached moose body fibers. Wood duck flank or Zelon® fibers may be used.

Abdomen: Egg Yarn®, chopped, yellow with added orange and chartreuse

Wing: Snowshoe hare's-foot

Thorax: Same as abdomen

Tying Notes: Similar to Fuzzball. The tail should be long. Wood duck flank fibers may be substituted to create a Dun-Emerger.

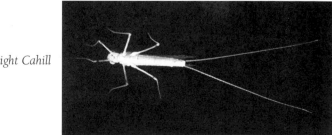

Light Cahill

57

Chapter 6–Two-Fly Systems

Subsurface/Subsurface Fly

The Egg Fly indicator has already been discussed.

Most often a larger weighted nymph or scud is tied in front of a small nymph or soft hackle. At times the upper fly is used primarily for weight. Tippets can be heavier, often 5x to 4x or 6x to 5x. Strike indicators are used approximately an arm's span above the upper fly. A deadly early season combination is a large weighted scud imitation with a trailing San Juan Worm.

Disadvantages of Two-Fly Systems

- Extra knots and rigging time.

- More tangles, especially when using 7x or when extra weight is added. Some tangles can be avoided by using stiffer tippet material, such as Maxima®. Most tangles result from casting errors. As previously mentioned, be sure to cast wide "soft" loops and let the backcast straighten before beginning the forward cast. (Remember that when casting with a dry-fly indicator, make the casts a bit short; don't forget the extra 18 to 24 inches of added tippet and fly.)

- Losing two flies at once to snags.

- Handling difficulty in wind and in tight quarters.

Cautions Regarding Two-Fly Systems

- Two-fly systems are not good if you have out-fished your attention span.

- If the fish are eating only one fly of a subsurface tandem, use only that fly.

- The number of foul-hooked fish increases.

CHAPTER 7
WINTER FISHING:
JANUARY THROUGH MID-MARCH

The period of January through mid-March is a good time to attend fly-fishing shows, tie necessary flies and maintain equipment. It is also an excellent time to fish. Short winter days mean fewer hours on the stream. In cold weather, however, that situation is not all bad.

Fly fishing for six hours in 25° F weather is not much of a problem if there is no wind. Shorter sessions at 22° F will work; but below these temperatures, tying flies is the best activity.

In winter the trout will be in the slow, deep water, and they will be sluggish. Feeding activity in water temperatures below 40° F will be extremely slow. At these temperatures trout take four to five days to digest a meal. As previously mentioned, the Driftless Area spring creeks receive a strong inflow of spring water at 48 to 50° F and maintain a relatively high winter temperature. These creeks do not freeze during the cold months. Additional warming by solar radiation and favorable air temperatures allow the fly angler to exploit trout feeding activity. Trout become less selective in winter because they have fewer food choices.

Plan your fishing session to match the warmest water temperature of the day, usually mid- or late afternoon. One of the best fishing periods is late afternoon, when shadows of neighboring bluffs fall over the stream. Also, fish sections of streams that have been warmed by solar radiation; such insects as scuds and water boatmen become more active in these areas. Portions of streams below a strong influx of spring water are likely to be productive. A rise in water temperature of only a few degrees may precipitate trout feeding activity. Conversely, falling water temperatures will diminish feeding activity. A warm winter day with a significant snow melt can rapidly reduce stream temperature, making fishing difficult. Additionally, melt water running into streams from plowed fields may turn a clear stream into "chocolate" in less than an hour. Pay attention to the amount of snow cover and the expected high temperatures in the area you plan to fish. The early days of a cold front similarly diminish feeding activity, although the fish may feed heavily in the period before the cold front settles in.

Proper cold weather gear is mandatory—and well known. Gore-Tex® and other breathable waders with appropriate wicking and insulating layers under-neath work very well. In extreme cold conditions, 4- to 5-mm neoprene bootfoot waders will keep feet tolerably warm. Felt soles are poor in snow because they rapidly become caked with snow and ice.

Carry two or three pairs of polypropylene gloves (I prefer fingerless), and place Grabber Mycoal® hand warmers in the gloves on the back of your hands.

Upper body gear of wicking and insulating garments with a waterproof, windproof, breathable shell, a neck gaiter and a hat with ear flaps completes the ensemble. Cold weather fishing experience will teach you that overdressing will hinder you as much as under dressing will.

I favor 8 1/2-foot or shorter rods during icing conditions because these rods have fewer line guides and because reaching the tip-top guide for de-icing is easy. A thin cork grip works well with gloves. Use a rod that you don't mind "swish-ing" back and forth in the stream to clear the rod of ice. (My only broken rods have been in cold conditions.)

Use old fly line that may be in need of replacement. Tippet material can be somewhat heavier in winter because the trout have not experienced as much fish-ing pressure. Heavier tippet material means fewer re-ties.

Having a large number of fly patterns for winter fishing is unnecessary. Leech, scud and midge imitations are always effective. In streams with stone fly popula-tions, dark stone fly nymphs from size 10 to size 20 are important.

"Dry-fly fishing with an adult stone fly pattern is great fun on a winter afternoon. The trout are not particularly selective about pattern; even a Black Caddis imitation will work."

Black Caddis imitation, left; natural black stone fly, right.

Black Stone Fly Nymph

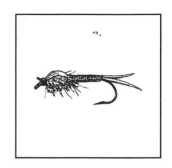

Hook: TMC® 3761—size 16, 18, 20

Thread: UNI-Thread®, black 8-0

Weight: 5 turns of .015 on size 16

Tail: Goose biots, 2, black

Abdomen: Tying thread over biots

Thorax: Black squirrel body fur

Wing case: Goose biots, butt ends of tail

Tying Notes: Crimp the barb and add weight. Start tying thread, and tie in the biot tails together, one on each side of the hook (flat sides vertical) with tips of the tail facing out (see Diagram 4, page 31). Wind thread to cover the forward extension of both tail biots to create the abdomen. Stand the butt end of biots vertically to be used later as a wing case; then dub a pronounced thorax. Pull both biots over the thorax, tie them off and whip finish. (Tie a few in smaller sizes without weight.)

Fishing Notes:

True to their name, stone fly nymphs favor the rocky, riffled stream sections (see Color Plate 8). Their presence can be determined by simple inspection of the cobbles. The nymphs crawl to bankside logs and stones, where emergence takes place. Their nymphal shucks are easily seen on these structures. Adults hatch from February to April, with females returning to the riffles for egg-laying. Even a sparse number of adults will elicit feeding activity by trout. The riseform is "caddislike."

Standard nymphing techniques in the riffles are effective. Also, allow the imitation to drift, then swing to the bank. Use the larger sizes for fishing the riffles and runs and the smaller sizes for fish you have seen in shallow water. Dry-fly fishing with an adult pattern is great fun on a winter afternoon. The trout are not particularly selective about pattern; even a Black Caddis imitation will work (see photo, page 60). A more specific pattern is the Black Stone Fly Adult.

Black Stone Fly Adult

Hook: TMC® 102Y—size 15, 17, 19

Thread: UNI-Thread®, black 8-0

Abdomen: Ultra-chenille, black, extended

Hackle: Black

Wing: Deer hair, black

Tying Notes: Crimp the barb; start the thread, leaving a tag end, and take it to the hook bend. Tie in an ultra-chenille "tail"; then advance the thread over the forward extension of the ultra-chenille, leaving room for the wing, which will be tied in "elk hair caddis style." Tie in the hackle, and palmer it to the hook bend. Secure the hackle with forward wraps of the tag end. Trim the hackle flat on the bottom and top. Stack the deer hair wing, and secure it with several wraps of thread. Whip finish on the bare hook just behind the hook eye. Snip the butt ends of the wing, leaving a small "head" extension. Burn the chenille tail extension to a taper as is done with the San Juan Worm.

Baetis nymphs are commonly found in stomach pump samplings of winter-caught trout. Hatching Baetis duns with rising trout are common in February. My notes of February 9, 1998, on the Spring Branch near Manchester, Iowa, include, "Good Baetis hatch today—fish were on top taking duns." Conditions were cloudy with a high of 40° F. Baetis patterns will be presented in the next chapter.

As noted earlier, the mainstay winter patterns are leeches, scuds and midges. Leech patterns in black, olive and gray, size 6, tied as previously noted (see page 27), are fished in the deep, slow pools. Cast to the head of the pool, and allow the Leech to settle on the bottom. A twitch or two on the descent may attract the attention of the trout. Retrieving the Leech should be "painfully slow." Most of the time, the imitation should be resting on the bottom with only brief movements imparted by the retrieve. I watched Tom Wendelburg hook and land a 22-inch brown trout using exactly this technique on an outing in early February (see Color Plate 8).

Scud patterns are useful year-round but especially in winter. The naturals become active, along with the trout, as stream temperatures warm. If the trout are taking size 28 and smaller minutiae in clear water, try a size 16 Gray Scud on 6x tippet "dribbled" along the bottom. Scud imitations are particularly effective in deep pools, slowly dead-drifted near the bottom with an occasional twitch.

In the winter, midges present an opportunity to match the hatch with surface and film patterns. They hatch daily on our coulee area streams. Most are dark, either black or gray, and can be as large as size 18. Good conditions for midging include a cloudy day without wind and with clear water. Most trout routinely begin their feeding day on midge larvae, switching later to scuds or Baetis nymphs as these insects become active. When the midges begin to hatch, the attention of the trout will be drawn to ascending pupae, pupae in the film and adults on the surface. I have seen some very sizable trout feeding on midges during the winter months.

In my book *Upper Midwest Flies That Catch Trout and how to fish them*, I have presented a collection of midge patterns from larvae through adults. Although I do not plan to re-present these flies, important patterns will be reviewed and new patterns added.

Tan Midge Larva

Hook: TMC® 200 R—size 20, Daiichi® 1140—size 20

Thread: UNI-Thread®, light yellow 8-0

Body: Antron® dubbing, tan

Rib: Fine gold

Tying Notes: Very easy. Start the thread and tie in the ribbing. Form a dubbing loop, add Antron® thinly, and twist it. Run the dubbing forward to create a body of uniform thickness. Advance the dubbing and tie it off.

Vinyl Rib Larva

Hook: TMC® 2487—size 20

Thread: UNI-Thread®, tan, olive, red, light yellow 8-0

Body: Tying thread overwrapped with vinyl rib, small, clear

Tying Notes: Start the thread and wrap it back and forth several times, extending it well down the hook bend. Firmly tie in the vinyl on top of the hook 1/4 shank-length behind the hook eye. Wrap the thread over the vinyl well down the hook bend while applying tension on the ribbing to stretch and thin it. Rewrap the thread several times over the shank, ending at the hook eye. Wind the vinyl rib tightly forward, and tie it off at the hook eye. Tint the head wraps brown with a marking pen.

Olive Biot Bow-Tie Pupa

Hook: Daiichi® 1140—size 20, 22

Thread: UNI-Thread®, olive 8-0

Abdomen: Goose biot, olive

Thorax: Snowshoe hare's-foot fibers

Tying Notes: Start tying the thread, and wind it well down the hook bend. Tie in the biot near the tip, and advance the thread to the thorax area. Wind the biot forward to create the abdomen, and tie it off. Snip a small bunch of hare's-foot fibers, and tie down "figure-of-eight" style in the thorax area (as if tying in poly spinner wings). Whip finish; then snip the "wings" about 1 mm from the base on each side.

Dark Midge Pupa

Hook: Daiichi® 1140—size 20

Thread: UNI-Thread®, black 8-0

Abdomen: Krystal Flash®, black

Wing Case: Antron® fibers, white

Thorax: CDC fibers

Tying Notes: Start the thread, and tie in Krystal Flash® well down the hook bend. Advance the thread to the thorax position, wind Krystal Flash® forward to thorax and tie it off. Tie in a small amount of Antron® fibers to be used as a wing case; then dub CDC fibers to the thread, and create a plump thorax. Pull the wing case over the thorax, and tie it down. Whip finish. Snip forward-protruding Antron®, leaving a short amount extending over the hook eye.

CDC Downwing Midge Adult

Hook: TMC® 101—size 24, 26

Thread: UNI-Thread®, rusty dun 8-0

Abdomen: Beaver, gray

Rib: Tying thread, tag end

Hackle: Grizzly

Wing: CDC fibers, natural gray

Tying Notes: Crimp the barb. Start the thread, leaving a tag end for the ribbing. Dub the beaver, and create a thin abdomen. Tie in the hackle, and wind it back to the hook bend. Advance the ribbing thread to secure the hackle, and tie it off. Use one CDC feather, and tie it in so that the fibers extend to the hook end. Snip the feather just ahead of the tie-in point. Whip finish. Note: It is possible to get two or three wings from one CDC feather; simply keep working down the quill.

Midge Cripple (Skating Midge)

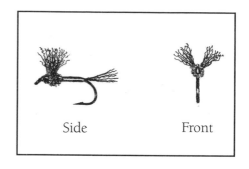

Side   Front

Hook: TMC® 920—size 20

Thread: UNI-Thread®, rusty dun 8-0

Shuck: Zelon®, rust

Abdomen: Tying thread

Thorax: Beaver, dark brown or black

Wing: Zelon® fibers, white

Tying Notes: Crimp the barb. Start tying the thread, and tie in the tail. Form an abdomen by wrapping the thread over forward-protruding shuck fibers. Tie in the wings with figure-of-eight wraps, spinner wing style; then elevate the wings to 15 degrees above horizontal with thread wraps. Dub the beaver, and wrap the thorax, crisscrossing between the wings. Whip finish.

Fishing Notes:

Midge Larvae may be fished deep, usually trailing a larger nymph, or fished near the surface, trailing an indicator dry fly. Tan and dark olive are the colors most often seen in pumped stomach contents. As the weather warms, trout will often be feeding on midge larvae in the flat water just above the riffles, especially in the mornings. A size 22 Brassie or a tan or olive Vinyl Rib Larva fished singly with an indicator is often effective.

I often fish the Dark Midge Pupa deep, behind a larger nymph. My friend Dick Ward often fishes a midge emerger (he favors a Loop-Wing Emerger, size 20 or 22) in the same fashion. It is remarkable how often the trout take the smaller fly. The Olive Biot Bow-Tie Pupa is best fished in the film to "bulging" trout when no surface insects are apparent. Add a small amount of floatant to the hare's-foot fibers, and fish the Pupa trailing a dry-fly indicator. The Olive Biot Bow-Tie Pupa is also an excellent fly to use when trout are taking tiny blue winged olive nymphs and emergers near the surface.

The CDC Downwing Midge has proved to be an excellent addition to the adult midge patterns presented in *Upper Midwest Flies That Catch Trout and how to fish them.* The CDC Downwing Midge floats well, is very visible and is well accepted by trout rising to midges (and small caddis in warmer months).

The Midge Cripple is a pattern shown to me by Bill Stark of Wabasha, Minnesota. He has guided for years on Wisconsin's Rush River. This fly pattern represents a "stuck-in-the-shuck" midge and is fished down and across, with movement, to trout that have been seen. Bill notes that the fly is at its best in February and March. He applies floatant to the wings, casts the fly above the fish, allows it to drift near the fish, "skates" it upstream a bit, then lets it drift past the trout. Bill notes, "The trout don't reject the Skating Midge."

In early April, I have seen beetles crawling across the snow!

CHAPTER 8
EARLY SEASON FISHING: MID-MARCH THROUGH MAY

Spring comes early to the Driftless Area. My streamside notes regularly record the first appearance of bluebirds, killdeer and woodcock in the first days of March. Wildflowers, such as bloodroot, hepatica and other spring ephemerals, appear in early April. Prime time for apple blossoms in the orchards of Gays Mills, Wisconsin, and La Crescent, Minnesota, is the first week of May. The trout begin feeding actively, and some of the best insect hatches of the year occur during the early season.

The progression of spring is often interrupted by snow and cold. Rain and wind are to be expected. Early spring rains, before the frost has left the ground and before vegetation is removing soil moisture, may account for rapidly rising stream levels. Runoff over fall-plowed unplanted fields can turn a clear stream to mud within an hour. One "bad" plowed field may be all that is needed to muddy a stream; moving above the field may be all that is necessary to find clear water (see Color Plate 10). My friend Norm Zimmerman and I looked at a lower section of Rush Creek near Rushford, Minnesota, after a spring downpour and found the water clear. Thinking that we were in luck, we drove upstream for 10 minutes to a stretch we wanted to fish and again found it clear. As we were preparing to fish, muddy water from upstream reduced the clarity to zero. We then drove down to the initial lower section and had nearly three hours of excellent dry-fly action (caddis and beetles) before the muddy water caught up to us.

Rainstorms in the coulee country can be very local; a stream in one valley can be "blown-out," while a neighboring stream in the next valley remains clear. Learning which streams tend to stay clear after a significant rainfall is important. Usually these streams lie in headwater areas with healthy watersheds. Knowing which streams are "intolerant" of rain will save you driving time.

For up-to-the-hour information about rainfall amounts and stream flows, use the Internet and access the Wisconsin district of the U.S.G.S. home page at http://wwwdwimdn.er.usgs.gov. Rainfall and stream flow amounts are available for many sites in southwest Wisconsin. Corresponding information for Iowa and Minnesota is available at the same Web site via links.

Reading clouded water in streams with which you are unfamiliar can be difficult. Fish near the base of large bankside willows, fish the pools just below narrowed sections of streams and fish next to any bank that borders deep water. One advantage of muddiness is that you can get close to fish without their seeing you.

The importance of home waters increases under dirty water conditions. The more home water you have, the better. Knowing the location of holding water, subsurface hazards and unproductive areas is very helpful. I took a 20-inch brown trout from "featureless" muddy water only because I had seen the fish next to a submerged rock under clear conditions a day earlier.

Rainy periods after the frost has left the ground may result in large numbers of earthworms being washed into the water. Consider using a San Juan Worm at this time, particularly if you noticed earthworms on the wet blacktop as you drove to the stream. Black Leeches and Sculpins, previously discussed, are excellent patterns for dirty water. Remember to clean your fly lines after fishing under these conditions.

Windy conditions are common during the early season. If heavy winds are expected, fish early in the day, before the wind increases. Breezes often begin about 8 a.m., and by midafternoon the wind is at its maximum. Evenings are frequently calm. High streaky clouds, often associated with wind, commonly call for subsurface fishing. On the other hand, low dense clouds, often associated with calmer conditions, many times produce surface activity.

During windy periods look for a sheltering valley or bluff. Try to fish with the wind at your back. Try to relax in the wind. Use a rod with enough stiffness to handle the wind. Shorten the leader, and use a strong tippet. Strong tippets are useful when a gust has blown the fly into bankside vegetation. During a wind gust, try to leave the fly on the water; then pick up the fly when the gust has abated.

When casting into the wind, pick up the line low off the water, lift high on the backcast and then drive the forward cast low. If you can cast with each hand, use the downwind hand in a crosswind. Wind markedly affects fine tippets. One advantage of wind, however, is that it ripples the surface, obscuring the line and the leader on the water.

Some of the most concentrated hatches of the year, particularly Baetis and the Brachycentrus caddis, occur during the early season and are found on all coulee region streams. Dark stone flies and midges persist. Hendricksons and sulphurs hatch during this time. Yellow crane flies and Stenonemas begin. Beetles and ants become important.

Baetis, which hatch under certain conditions in all months, occur most

COLOR PLATE 9

Hendrickson Spinner
p. 79

Yellow Crane Fly Adult
p. 81

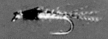

Tiny Olive Nymph
p. 87

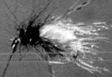

Tan Caddis Pupa
p. 88

Bob's Teardrop Emerger
p. 89

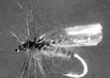

Tan Caddis Adult
p. 89

Brown Hackle Peacock
Caddis
p. 90

Black Foam Beetle
p. 91

Black Glass-Bead Head
Beetle
p. 91

Pass Ant
p. 92

COLOR PLATE 10

"One bad plowed field may be all that is needed to muddy a stream; moving above the field may be all that is necessary to find clear water."

"Stomach pump samplings collected on a coulee stream in late April between 8 a.m. and 2:30 p.m. revealed and confirmed the natural progression of the Black Caddis hatch. Early morning samples consisted almost entirely of larvae."

This brown trout took an Olive Larva.

Waterloo Creek (Allamakee County, Iowa) in April during the Brachycentrus Caddis hatch period.

Check streamside cobwebs for the "hatch of the day."

Crane Fly adult

"Rainfall in September, with rising stream flows, may draw very large brown trout into small tributary streams. Such streams abound in the Driftless Area and are located by studying maps. Fishing these tributaries at the proper time may result in your largest trout of the season."

Photo by Fred Young

"During midday, fish the shaded side of any available cover, such as weed beds, bank runs and overhanging willows." Paul Mueller plays a 16-inch brown trout that took an ant pattern presented along a shaded bank beneath an overhanging willow.

heavily in early spring. Look for these size 16 through 20 "blue-winged olives" on cold, gray days. If the night has been cold with frost in the morning, Baetis usually begin hatching between 11 a.m. and 2 p.m. Following a warm night, hatches occur between 9 and 11 a.m. Baetis duns are size 16 through 20, have two tails and tiny hind wings. Tiny olives (formerly Pseudocloeon), which begin hatching as soon as late May, are size 22-26, have two tails and no hind wings. Paraleptophlebia duns, which occur in mid-April to May, are slightly larger and darker than Baetis, have three tails and prominent hind wings. Use the same series of flies, deep and surface nymphs, emergers, duns and spinners—in appropriate sizes—for all these insects.

For deeply fished nymphs, use the Olive Nymph (described in *Upper Midwest Flies That Catch Trout and how to fish them*) or the Pheasant Tail (P.T.) Nymph (Weighted Variant).

Pheasant Tail Nymph (Weighted Variant)

Hook: TMC® 9300—size 14-20
Daiichi®1550—size 14-20

Thread: UNI-Thread®, camel 8-0

Weight: .010, 6 turns for size 18

Tail: Pheasant tail

Abdomen: Tying thread over pheasant tail

Rib: Copper wire, fine

Wing case: Goose biot, rust

Thorax: Australian opossum, brown or rust

Tying Notes: Crimp the barb, and add weight in the thorax area. Start the tying thread and secure the lead. Take tying thread to the hook bend, and tie in the tail about 1/2-shank length. Advance the thread over the anteriorly protruding pheasant tail fibers to the "thorax lead." Reverse the thread, and start winding (one or two wraps) toward the hook bend. Tie in the rib; then bend back the pheasant tail fibers over the hook shank. Continue winding back the thread to the hook bend, including the rib and fibers. Readvance the thread to the thorax, pull the pheasant tail fibers over the shank and secure them in the thorax area with the thread. Wind the rib forward to the thorax; tie off and snip both the pheasant tail fibers and the rib. (Make sure the pheasant tail fibers stay on top of the hook shank when winding the rib.) Tie in the biot, which will be pulled over the thorax later. Dub a pronounced thorax, pull over the biot and secure it with 10 or 12 wraps of thread; then whip finish on the bare hook just behind the eye. Snip the biot butt. Pick out the thorax fibers.

I no longer use "standard" P. T. nymphs. I prefer this variant pattern because there is no compromise of the hook gap. Also, the abdomen is kept very thin as in the naturals, and durability is much improved. For an even more durable imitation, use stacked moose body hair instead of pheasant tail. Even red squirrel tail fibers will work. The pattern can be tied as a bead head by omitting the lead and the wing case. Just add an abdomen and a touch of Australian opossum behind the bead.

The color of the P. T. Variant Nymph is easily altered by using different thread colors and dyed pheasant tail fibers, especially black and olive. The pattern may be tied as a flashback by substituting mylar for the biot wing case.

This fly and the Olive Nymph (see *Upper Midwest Flies That Catch Trout and how to fish them*) are my two most-used deeply fished patterns for Baetis, Paraleptophlebia and various "sulphurs." Size 18 is the most commonly used size.

For nymphs in the film and just below the surface, use the Blue-Winged Olive (BWO) Floating Nymph or a simple Two Biot Nymph.

Two-Biot Nymph

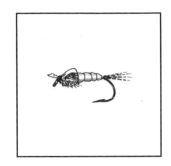

Hook: TMC® 100—size 18, 20

Thread: UNI-Thread®, rusty dun 8-0

Tail: Wood duck flank (short)

Abdomen: Goose biot, olive

Wing case: Goose biot, olive

Thorax: Hare's-foot fibers, chopped

Tying Notes: This simple pattern is tied in the order of the listed components. For the abdomen, tie in the biot by the tip; then wind it forward. A second biot is used for the wing case. Make sure that the thorax is pronounced and picked out. Whip finish on the bare hook just behind the hook eye.

Emerger patterns include both the Fuzzball (see page 56) tied in size 18 and 20 and used primarily as an indicator dry fly and the Shillinglaw Emerger.

Shillinglaw Emerger

Hook: TMC® 100—size 18, 20, TMC® 101—size 22

Thread: UNI-Thread®, rusty dun 8-0

Tail: Wood duck flank fibers

Abdomen: Beaver, olive-gray

Rib: Krystal Flash®, pearlescent (optional)

Wing: Antron® yarn, fluorescent white, gray or black

Thorax: Australian opossum, brown

Tying Notes: This simple pattern is again tied in the order of the listed components. Make sure that the wing is full enough for easy visibility. The wing extends back over the fly to the base of the tail. The thorax is tied in front of the wing and is moderately pronounced.

For duns on the surface, I use the BWO Parachute described in Upper Midwest Flies That Catch Trout and how to fish them, *almost exclusively with fluorescent white or black wing posts. Use the white post for dark water backgrounds and the black post for light water backgrounds. When tying parachute patterns, be sure to tie long split tails. The abdomens should be thin, and the bottom of the fly should be flat without even one fiber protruding downward. Wing posts of turkey flat, Hi Vis® or Lureflash Antron Body Wool® should be just a bit short. The hackle should be slightly oversized for the hook size.*

Female Baetis crawl beneath the surface to deposit their eggs. Spinner patterns, therefore, are less important than they are for tiny olives, sulphurs, tricos and others.

Fishing Notes:

Frank Sawyers, in his book *Nymphs and the Trout*, notes that deep-lying trout within view of the fly fisher are generally watching the bottom and are taking nymphs from an area about four feet in front and to either side. Trout near the surface are looking for food just above them, and the area for taking is much smaller. The author states, "The midwater fish is the easiest victim; his eyes are watching everywhere, even behind him." These words should guide your efforts when fishing to trout within view. Seen at the surface, fish with tipping head-tail rises are almost certainly taking emerging duns or nymphs wiggling near the surface. If these fish are keying on the "micro-wiggle" of a nymph, they can be very difficult to take. For these fish I often use the Fuzzball indicator (emerger) and a Two Biot Nymph (surface nymph) in combination. The Olive Biot Bow-Tie Pupa (see page 64) is also useful as a trailing fly in this situation. The Shillinglaw Emerger fished singly, often a size smaller than the natural, is very reliable for fish at the surface. Also, see Tom Wendelburg's Trailing Shuck Baetis (page 105). As mentioned, the parachute pattern is my favorite when trout are on the duns. Remember that Frank Sawyers also observed that if fish are taking duns, they will take nymphs even better.

The Brachycentrus (Grannom, black caddis) hatch offers perhaps the best dry-fly fishing of the year. A reasonable estimate of the trout population of a stream may be made when the fish are rising to pupae and adults at the surface.

Brachycentrus caddis are case builders. If you see the brown chimney cases attached to rocks and branches beneath the surface of any stream, you will know that a hatch will occur in April. The larvae in the cases are green to olive. Pupae have abdomens of light olive to green (Borger Color System® 24, 30) with dark heads, legs and "wings." The adults have charcoal-colored bodies and wings (Borger Color System® 108, 114) and are size 16 through 19.

The earliest hatching date, with rising fish, that I have encountered was April 6. Hatching is usually well under way by April 20. The hatch continues into May, then dwindles.

Brachycentrus imitations include the Peeking Caddis, Olive Larva, Brachycentrus Pupa and Brachycentrus Adult. Larvae and pupae of the natural are usually larger than the adult.

*If fish are taking Duns, they
will take Nymphs even better.*

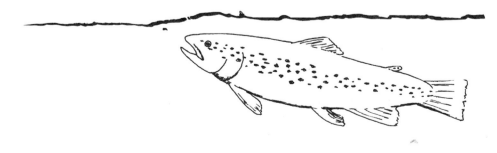

Olive Larva

Hook: TMC® 2457—size 14

Thread: UNI-Thread®, olive 8-0

Head: Glass bead, black—size 11-0

Weight: .015 lead, 7 turns

Abdomen: Antron® dubbing, medium olive

Rib: Silver wire, small

Thorax: Hare's Ear Plus®, black

Tying Notes: Crimp the barb, and add the bead and lead. Wind the thread well back on the hook bend, and tie in the ribbing material. Form a dubbing loop, add the Antron and then dub the body. Advance the ribbing; then dub a bit of Hare's Ear Plus® just behind the bead. Tie it off and brush with Velcro.

Brachycentrus Pupa

Hook: TMC® 2487 –size 14

Thread: UNI-Thread®, olive 8-0

Abdomen: Antron® dubbing, kelly green mixed with fluorescent chartreuse rabbit

Rib: UNI-Thread®, black 3-0

Wing: Swiss straw, charcoal

Legs: Duck wing covert feather, dark gray

Head: Hare's Ear Plus®, black

Tying Notes: Crimp the barb, start the thread and take well back on the hook bend. Tie in the ribbing, form a dubbing loop, add the dubbing and wind the abdomen. Advance the ribbing, and tie it off. Brush the abdomen with Velcro. Tie in a ventral wing (beard fashion) of Swiss straw at the thorax position (unfold a strip of Swiss straw, and use 1/4 of width, folded). Wind one turn of covert feather, dub the head, brush back with Velcro and whip finish.

Brachycentrus Adult

Hook: TMC® 100—size 16, 18.
TMC® 102Y—size 17, 19

Thread: UNI-Thread®, black 8-0

Abdomen: Antron®, gray and black mixed

Wing: Swiss straw, charcoal

Thorax: Same as abdomen

Hackle: Black

Tying Notes: My most-used hook is the TMC® 102Y, size 17. Crimp the barb, start the thread, take it to hook bend, add the dubbing and wind a thin abdomen. Select a 1-inch section of Swiss straw. Unfold it. Cut the unfolded Swiss straw parallel to the crinkles into three equal strips. Fold one of the strips, moisten it with your tongue and tie it in 1/4-shank length behind the hook eye. Trim to a caddis shape. Tie in the hackle, add thorax dubbing and wind the hackle in front of the wing. Whip finish.

Fishing Notes:

Stomach pump samplings collected on a coulee stream in late April between 8 a.m. and 2:30 p.m. revealed and confirmed the natural progression of the hatch. Early morning samples consisted almost entirely of larvae (see Color Plate 10). By 10 a.m. pupae were present. Adult black caddis flies were on the water by 11 a.m. with rising trout. Excellent dry-fly fishing continued for nearly three hours. The largest fish landed was a 17-inch brown, which contained both pupae and adults. This fish was feeding in the quiet water below a riffle. Feeding activity usually stops abruptly with an ensuing afternoon lull. Later in the afternoon sporadic risers contained black ants and small black beetles.

Winter fishing requires slow, drag-free drifts of the fly. As spring and summer arrive, adding movement to the imitation often increases success. This adjustment is particularly important with caddis imitations. To match the behavior of the natural and to gain the attention of the trout, twitch and swing the pupal and adult patterns in the current.

Spent caddis need to be fished dead drift and flush in the film. Modify the wing of the Brachycentrus Adult by trimming the hackle on the bottom, splitting the wing down the middle and then pressing a wing off to each side of the fly so that each wing floats flush in the film.

Peeking Caddis imitations, which represent the encased larva, are more often useful in October, November and December because stomach contents at that time often reveal cased caddis. A Bead Head Pheasant Tail Nymph works just as well.

Ephemerella subvaria, or the Hendrickson, is not as well distributed in coulee area streams as Baetis or Brachycentrus are. Some streams—such as Trout Run in Winona and Fillmore Counties, Minnesota, French Creek in Iowa and the Rush River in Wisconsin—have reliable hatches. Many streams have sporadic, segmental activity, and some streams do not support the insects. Chasing Hendricksons can be futile at times.

The earliest date on which I have recorded the duns as trout stomach contents is March 26, 1998, on Iowa's French Creek. In that year the hatch was nearly finished in coulee area streams by mid-April. Usually hatching begins in mid-April and extends through May. Duns emerge in midafternoon, and spinners fall in the evening.

Imitations include dark hare's-ear-type nymphs, flush-floating emerger patterns, parachutes and spinners. All are tied in size 14.

Please see page 103 for a Hendrickson Dun Emerger pattern and fishing notes by Walt Coaty. An effective spinner pattern follows.

Hendrickson Spinner

Hook: TMC® 100–size 14

Thread: UNI-Thread®, brown 8-0

Tail: Moose body hair, long, split

Egg sac: Antron® dubbing, light yellow (optional)

Abdomen: Tying thread, over butt ends of tail

Wing: Twinkle organza (available from fabric stores; also known as Spinner-Glass® in fly shops)

Thorax: Australian opossum, brown

Tying Notes: This is a straightforward tie. Tie in the order of the listed components. The optional egg sac is a tiny ball at the base of the tail. Crisscross the thorax dubbing over the wing tie-in area.

Fishing Notes:

Standard nymphing techniques are used before the duns appear. Swinging a nymph or a dark soft hackle may be very effective.

In the evening, when you see the female insects silhouetted against the sky with their egg sac-holding abdomens curled beneath them, you may expect excellent fishing in the quiet water below the riffles. This is a good time to head to the location of a previously discovered large trout.

The hatching of sulphurs on coulee streams is not as universal as the hatching of Baetis and Brachycentrus. Some streams exhibit excellent activity, while others have only sparse hatches. Even on a stream with a good hatch, activity may be segmental.

Three important species are present: size 14 and 16 Ephemerella rotonda and invaria (these insects are known as "Light Hendricksons" in some regions) and size 18 Ephemerella dorothea. Rotonda appears in early to mid-May and lasts for a few weeks. Invaria begins somewhat later and lasts well into June. Dorothea hatches in mid- to late May and lasts through June.

The insects prefer gray afternoons for hatching. Wind and cold do not seem to deter them. I have watched the brown nymphs rise to the surface in quiet water, rest at the surface and then develop a dorsal split at the thorax through which the yellow dun emerges. If you are having difficulty taking fish on yellow dun imitations, try a size 16 brown floating nymph.

My friend John Shillinglaw, while fishing Timber Coulee on May 24, 1999—an overcast, windy day—noted that the sulphur duns appeared about 3 p.m. Rising trout were taken on a size 16 Sparkle Dun, and initial pumped stomach contents revealed fat, brown size 16 nymphs. The hatch ended at 5:30 p.m.

Spinner imitations are very important for all sulphur species. In the mornings on quiet water, do not forget "washed-up" Rusty Spinners, size 14 and 16, tied with twinkle organza wings. As an example, I took several trout on Camp Creek (Fillmore County, Minnesota) between 8 and 9 a.m. in quiet water on a size 14 Rusty Spinner. Streamside cobwebs had captured scores of the naturals.

The series of fly patterns for sulphurs is similar to that of Baetis and includes Pheasant Tail and brown/olive/yellow nymphs, both weighted and unweighted; the yellow Fuzzball with a trailing shuck of rusty brown Zelon®; parachutes; Sparkle Duns (Borger Color System® 48 with a bit of orange in the thorax); and Rusty Spinners. See also the "Contributing Experts" chapter for a Sulphur Dun-Emerger (page 103) by Walt Coaty and a Sulphur Dun (page 106) by Tom Wendelburg.

Yellow crane fly adults, and occasionally the larvae, are very important trout insects on all streams of the Driftless Area. Crane flies, along with midges, belong to the order Diptera. Adult crane flies are mosquitolike with thin clear wings and very long legs (see Color Plate 12). The most common color on our coulee area streams is light yellow, although some insects are tan to light brown.

Aquatic crane fly larvae resemble maggots; most are cream colored. The larvae move to stream margins, and pupae develop in the soil from which the adults emerge.

Yellow crane fly adults remain close to the stream; their fluttering close to the surface resembles caddis. Females land on the surface, then flutter to bankside rocks and vegetation to lay their eggs.

My streamside notes show the presence of adults as soon as late April. Emergence continues steadily into the fall, with periods of heavy activity in May and June. Crane flies are commonly on the water with the sulphurs, tiny Baetis, yellow stone flies and tan caddis. Often, however, the only surface insects are crane flies.

Even small numbers of the naturals will initiate feeding activity by trout. If you see occasional fluttering crane flies and isolated splashy rises, try the Yellow Crane Fly Adult. Mark single rises accurately. Select a landmark, and carefully fix the trout's location. This practice is especially important if you need to move several yards upstream before casting.

My notes of May 19, 1999, recorded on Timber Coulee, describe pumped stomach contents consisting of Baetis and tiny Olive nymphs and two yellow crane fly adults. The only two rises of the trout were to crane flies. On May 27 on the West Fork of the Kickapoo, stomach contents showed yellow and brown caddis pupae (some still alive) and a few yellow crane fly adults. Again, the trout rose only to crane flies.

When large numbers of crane flies are fluttering over the surface, the trout might be very selective toward them, even in the presence of other insects such as sulphur duns. Crane flies on the surface will have their wings flat in the film; sulphur duns ride with their wings up.

Yellow Crane Fly Adult

Hook: TMC® 100—size 18

Thread: UNI-Thread®, light cahill 8-0

Abdomen: Beaver, light yellow

Wing: Dry-fly hackle feathers, white

Hackle: White—size 2

Thorax: Beaver or rabbit, orange

Tying Notes: Dub a very thin abdomen, starting well down the hook bend and continuing forward to 1/4-shank length behind the hook eye. The anterior abdomen should end in a slight ball. Tie in the wing "delta style" just ahead of the ball, and splay it outward with 1 turn of thread behind each wing. Wings should extend well beyond the abdomen. Tie in the grossly oversized hackle; then dub the thorax. Take three winds of hackle over the thorax and tie off. Trim the bottom fibers and touch with orange felt-tip marker.

Fishing Notes:

This pattern is useful on all coulee region streams, beginning in late April and continuing for months. As mentioned, the imitation is particularly useful for the occasional riser in the presence of occasional naturals. The Yellow Crane Fly Adult is also effective in the evenings because of its excellent visibility. Small trout will "bump" it and often not be hooked. Large trout will take it with authority.

CHAPTER 9
SUMMER FISHING:
JUNE THROUGH SEPTEMBER

Despite the heat of summer, most Driftless Area streams maintain trout-favorable temperatures. For example, in late June 1999 at 3:30 p.m. on a middle section of Waterloo Creek (Allamakee County, Iowa), the air temperature was 89° F, and the stream temperature was 66° F. Small light-yellow midges were on the surface, and trout were dimpling.

By this time, streams are likely to be low and clear, and the heavily fished trout have become well educated.

During hot spells, try to fish early in the morning; later, fish shaded areas. Lengthy sections of streams on the west side of bluffs may remain in shade until late morning. Conversely, streams flowing next to the east side of a bluff will be shaded by midafternoon. During midday, fish the shaded side of any available cover, such as weed beds, bank runs and overhanging willows (see Color Plate 12).

Move slowly in midday heat. Find shaded productive-appearing areas, and stay there for an hour or more; become part of the environment. As usual, "look first and cast second." Start fishing the pools with a nondisturbing surface fly; then work more deeply with more "intrusive" flies. Remember the advice "dark day, dark fly—light day, light fly." Look closely at the water immediately in front of you. In summer, trout often lie in small bankside recesses well away from the pools and riffles. If you make a bad cast, don't immediately rip it off the water. Rather, let the fly complete its drift; then recast.

Following long summer days, fishing after dark may result in the largest fish of the day.

Wooded, brushy and overgrown sections of streams offer shade (and terrestrials). Remember, the coulee country is very fertile. Weeds that would be three feet high in other regions are seven feet high here! Fishing the brush usually is worth the effort. Use a shorter rod and a heavier tippet. Fully palmered dry flies, such as the BHP Beetle (with downward protruding hackle fibers left intact) or the Hackle Wing Hopper, seldom hang up in the brush because the hackle fibers at the hook gap act like weed guards. You can cast and drape the leader over a branch or the grass, and the fly will slide right over. At times you have to take a chance and cast the dry fly in front of a bankside obstruction, producing either a trout or a snag. Room for back casts may be very limited. Sometimes in the brush, you are looking behind as often as ahead of yourself. If you have a back cast lane, project it forward to a landmark ahead; then line up your back cast with the landmark.

In the absence of back cast lanes, the roll cast becomes important. Dry flies must be very buoyant if much roll casting is done because you do not have the luxury of false casting the dry fly. A pattern incorporating foam might be necessary.

Fishing brushy areas allows evaluation of your striking technique. If you miss a strike and the fly ends up in the branches behind you, you are striking too hard!

Do not transmit vibrations into a pool by being heavy footed on a log that extends down into the pool. Consider fishing a Girdle Bug, Wooly Bugger or minnow imitation downstream under logs and brush that extend over the stream.

Fishing brushy streams presents the problem of getting back to your car at the end of a fishing session. Consider checking the section of stream by car beforehand. Note areas where the stream is close to the road; then exit the stream at that point. Many Iowa streams have "stocking roads," which parallel the stream and allow an easy exit route. Some streams, such as the Farmer Valley and Buffalo in Wisconsin and the Camp and Root in Minnesota, have sections bordering recreation trails.

June is known as a month of thunderstorms, and the presence of lightning can cause a dangerous situation. Despite the fact that trout feed heavily just before a storm, lightning may make this a poor time to be on the water. Most people struck by lightning are near water or under trees, and most are struck prior to or after the rain. Take action early enough to avoid being caught in the storm. When you see the lightning flash, count the seconds to the thunder and divide by five. This number gives the approximate distance in miles between you and the lightning. You are safest in a hard-topped automobile. Do not resume fishing too soon after the rain has ended. If you are caught onstream, take these actions:

- Get away from the water immediately.

- Set your graphite rod away from you, and stay away from metal fences.

- Avoid areas that are higher than the surrounding landscape; go to level or lower areas.

- Do not use a tree as a shelter.

- If you feel a tingling sensation, immediately crouch down and cover your ears. Do not lie down or place your hands on the ground.

Rainfall in September, with rising stream flows, may draw very large brown trout from the larger rivers into small tributary streams. Such streams abound in the Driftless Area and are located by studying maps. Fishing these tributaries at the proper time may result in your largest trout of the season (see Color Plate 12).

The major summer hatches, which appear on all coulee region streams daily, are the tiny olives, caddis species, terrestrials and midges.

Sulphurs continue through June, and Baetis may appear on suitable days, especially early and late in the period. Crane flies persist, along with light cahills and yellow stone flies. Tricos appear in July and continue through September on many streams. Hexagenia limbata hatches are limited to only a few streams. Isonychia species and Ephoron leukon appear in August and September in certain areas.

Beginning in mid- to late May and continuing into the fall, a daily hatch of tiny olives provides the spring creek angler with consistent fishing on all streams. The insect responsible for this activity is the bug formerly known as Pseudocloeon, a size 22 through 26 pale yellow/olive dun with two tails, medium gray wings and no hind wing. (Use a hand lens to aid visualization). The Pseudocloeon genus has been reclassified as Plauditus. May 19 is the earliest date on which I have recorded these tiny olives. Like small ants and tricos, tiny olives are small food items favored by trout.

The insects, for fly-fishing purposes, are reduced versions of Baetis vagans. The brown/olive-yellow nymphs are spear-shaped swimmers favoring oxygen-rich limestone streams. The nymphs tend to drift in the current both early and late in the day, making them readily available to trout. Emergence occurs in the surface film, and the duns ride the surface for long distances before taking off, molting and returning as spinners to the riffles.

All stages of the tiny olives (which often look like "tiny sulphurs") are important to the fly fisher. Hatching activity usually begins in mid- to late afternoon and continues into evening. Heavy hatches occasionally are encountered, but more often the duns just "dribble" along a few at a time.

As noted, this hatch is a "constant" for months in the coulee country. Pumped stomach contents reveal the extended presence of tiny olives:

May 19, 1999, evening, two brown trout, Spring Coulee (Vernon County, WI)

Tiny olive duns (many)

Tiny olive nymphs (many)

Black ant, size 18 (1)

Sulphur dun, size 18 (1)

Yellow crane fly adult (2)

June 7, 1999, morning and evening, multiple brown trout, Camp Creek (Fillmore County, MN)

Tiny olive spinners, size 22 (many)

Tiny olive nymphs (many)

Tiny olive duns (few)

Black ant, size 22 (1)

Baetis nymphs, size 18 (few)

Sulphur (Light Hendrickson) spinners, size 14 (few)

July 5, 1999, midafternoon-evening, two brown trout, Rush River (Pierce County, WI)

Tiny olive nymphs, emergers and duns (many)

No other insects

August 1, 1998, morning, two brown trout, Winnebago Creek (Houston County, MN)

Tiny olive nymphs (few)

Trico spinners (many)

Cased caddis, size 16 (few)

September 24, 1995, one brown trout, Timber Coulee (Vernon County, WI)

Tiny olive duns (many)

Gray scuds, size 14, 16 (few)

Red ants, size 22 (many)

Tiny olives are regularly found as stomach contents of trout from Iowa streams in October and November.

Imitative patterns include the nymph, Shillinglaw Emerger, Fuzzball, parachute and spinner. All are reduced versions of the Blue-Winged Olive series discussed earlier. Presented here is an effective nymph imitation.

COLOR PLATE 15

This 10-inch brown took a size 12 BHP Beetle.

This 14-inch brown took a size 10 Black Glass Bead Head Beetle the instant the fly hit the water.

COLOR PLATE 16

"In October, the display of autumn color on the bluffs and the migration of hawks and eagles along the Mississippi River are worth the trip."

Fred Young connects with, then releases, a large brown in October.

"Remember to wear blaze orange during the various hunting seasons."

John Shillinglaw is about to fish the waist-deep channels in the watercress.

(French Creek, Allamakee County, Iowa)

COLOR PLATE 13

  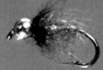

Mike's Gold Demon
p. 97

Mike's Gold-Stripe Hare's Ear
p. 98

Mike's Gold-Stripe
Caddis
p. 98

——————————(Tied by Mike Hogue)——————————

Flashback Black Wet Fly
p. 99

Root River Special
p. 101

P. G. Caddis
p. 102

(Tied by Tom Dornack) ————————(Tied by Wayne Bartz)————————

 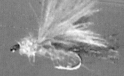 

Hendrickson Dun-Emerger
p. 103

Sulphur Dun-Emerger
p. 103

Sulphur Dun
p. 106

————————(Tied by Walt Coaty)————————   *(Tied by Tom Wendelburg)*

Trailing Shuck Baetis
p. 105
(Tied by Tom Wendelburg)

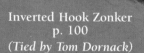

Inverted Hook Zonker
p. 100
(Tied by Tom Dornack)

Spring Coulee (Vernon County, Wisconsin).

Rush River
(Pierce County, Wisconsin).

Tiny Olive Nymph

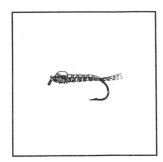

Hook: TMC® 101—size 22; TMC® 9300—size 20

Thread: UNI-Thread®, olive 8-0

Tail: Wood duck flank fibers. May also use various guard hairs, which are more durable.

Abdomen: Antron® dubbing, fine, light yellow-olive

Shell back/wing case: Goose biot, olive

Rib: Gold wire, fine

Thorax: Australian opossum, brown

Tying Notes: Crimp the barb, start the thread and wind to hook bend. Tie in the tail; advance the thread to midshank over tail butts. Snip the tail butts. Tie in the biot near the tip, butt facing the rear. Wind the thread back to the hook bend over the biot, including the rib. Dub an extremely thin abdomen, pull the biot over and secure it with two wraps of thread at the front of the abdomen. Stand up the biot to be used later as a wing case. Advance and secure the ribbing. Dub the thorax and pull it over the wing case. Secure the wing case behind the hook eye; whip finish on the bare hook just behind the hook eye. Snip the biot butt.

Fishing Notes: By June, you will notice the trout to be gaining weight and length. The 9-inch fish of the early season will be well on their way to becoming 12 and 13 inchers. Tiny olive patterns offer a better chance to hook large fish than the trico imitations do. Fish the nymph as part of a two-fly rig, either deep behind a large weighted nymph or just beneath the surface, supported by a size 18 or 20 Fuzzball.

The Shillinglaw Emerger (page 74) in sizes 22 and 24 is very effective in the film. Tie some with a bulky wing to aid visibility and floatation when used singly, and tie some with a wispy wing to be used as a trailing fly of a two-fly rig.

Under good lighting conditions, tiny olive duns are easily seen on the surface. In early summer they are often accompanied by much larger yellow crane flies, sulphurs, light cahills and yellow stone flies. Do not underestimate the power of a size 22 parachute. Often I will fish the parachute until evening, then switch to a larger, more visible fly, such as the Hare's-Foot Light Cahill, as evening progresses. Large trout become much easier late in the evening.

Tiny olive spinners are important in late afternoon and evening, especially on the smooth water at the tail end of pools and structures. In the morning, trout might be taking washed-up spinners in shallow eddies and slow, flat water. Look for faint rises with no apparent insects on the water. Often you can approach to within 15 or 20 feet of these fish. In this situation, 7x tippet and casting accuracy are vital. The first hooked fish or indelicate presentation will put down the risers for several minutes. Wait until the fish reappear, and try again. When feeding activity to spinners stops, try a terrestrial pattern such as a beetle.

Surface caddis activity is a daily occurrence on coulee area streams. The tan caddis (cinnamon caddis, spotted sedge) is the most common summer caddis. Smaller caddis flies with brown or green bodies and gray-brown wings will be encountered.

The tan caddis belongs to the Hydropsychidae family. The net spinning, wormlike larvae are dull yellow and live in protected recesses of subsurface rocks and branches. The pupae have a yellow abdomen and a brown thorax. Adults are camel colored. Emergence is in the evening and occurs from May into September.

Tying Notes: Except for color and size, all phases of the tan caddis—larva, pupa, emerger and adult—are tied exactly as the Brachycentrus patterns are. These Tan Caddis patterns may be summarized as follows:

Tan Caddis Larva

Tie this fly in size 14 and 16, and use tan dubbing for the abdomen, gold wire or tinsel for the rib and brown Hare's Ear Plus® dubbing for the thorax, behind a black glass bead.

Tan Caddis Pupa

This fly is also tied in size 14 and 16. Use a mixture of synthetic/natural fibers to approximate BCS® 50 for the abdomen, charcoal Swiss straw ventral "winglets," light brown soft hackle for legs and brown Australian opossum for the thorax.

Tan Caddis Emerger

Use a ginger Zelon® shuck and short dorsal hare's-foot wings. Also refer to

Carl Richards and Bob Braendle's *Caddis Super Hatches* for two excellent emergers: Bob's Tear Drop Emerger and Bob's Quick and Dirty Emerger. These patterns were designed on Michigan's Muskegon River but have universal applicability.

Tan Caddis Adult

Tie this pattern on a TMC® 100, size 16, and use an abdomen of natural camel dubbing. Ribbing with pearlescent Krystal Flash® is optional. Tie in a wing of tan Swiss straw, add a few wood duck flank fibers trailing from each side to mimic legs and then add a camel thorax and a ginger collar hackle.

Tan Caddis Spent Adult

Simply trim the bottom hackle fibers; then split the wing of an adult pattern, and press it so that it lies flat, half on each side.

Fishing Notes:
My most-used patterns on coulee area streams are the pupa and the adult.

The combination of adding weight to the Tan Caddis Pupa and drifting it deep often produces larger trout than a more superficial presentation does. The natural pupa is commonly found in pumped stomach contents. Samplings of three brown trout caught and released on the West Fork of the Kickapoo River during a late afternoon/evening in early June revealed these contents:

Tan caddis pupae, size 14, 16 (many, some still alive)
Tan Caddis shucks (few) (BCS® 91)
Yellow stone fly adults (2)
Yellow stone fly nymphs (few)
Yellow crane fly adults (2)
Black ant, winged, size 14 (1)

The fish taken in late afternoon ate the Tan Caddis Pupa; those in the evening took a size 14 Hare's-Foot Light Cahill (tied with a wood duck tail). As mentioned, this dry fly is an excellent pattern in low light conditions when large yellow insects are hatching (see page 57).

The Tan Caddis Adult may be fished in a variety of ways: dead drift, dead drift with "twitches," active retrieve, subsurface with action (for egg layers) or dead drift flush in the film (spent adults).

Also note the P.G. Caddis, a Wayne Bartz pattern described on page 102.

For other smaller caddis encountered on the surface, a generic pattern—the Brown Hackle Peacock Caddis—works well.

Brown Hackle Peacock Caddis

Hook: TMC® 102Y—size 19

Thread: UNI-Thread®, rusty brown 8-0

Abdomen: Peacock herl

Hackle: Brown

Wing: Elk or deer body hair, gray-brown

Tying Notes: Crimp the barb, start the thread and wrap to the hook bend. Tie in the peacock and hackle (butt end). Make a "rope" by tightly winding the peacock and hackle around the tying thread. Advance the rope almost to the hook eye to create an abdomen, leaving room to tie in the wing. Stack the elk hair, and tie it in just behind the hook eye. (The length of the wing extends to the hook bend.) Secure with a dozen wraps of thread, and whip finish on the bare hook just behind the hook eye. Trim the elk hair butts long enough to create the impression of a head.

Of the four major terrestrials, beetles have the longest period of usefulness, followed by ants, crickets and grasshoppers.

The BHP Beetle has already been discussed. This is a "searching" kind of dry fly that can be used most months of the year (see Color Plate 15).

Finicky spring and summer trout, however, often require a small beetle imitation "helplessly floating on the water with outstretched legs." The Black Foam Beetle has proved useful for these fish, particularly in slow currents and beneath trees.

Black Foam Beetle

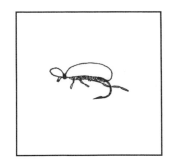

Hook: TMC® 102Y—size 19

Thread: UNI-Thread®, black 8-0

Shell back: Foam, black (a cross section approximately 1/8" x 3/16")

Abdomen: Peacock herl

Legs: Krystal Flash®, black

Tying Notes: Crimp the barb, start the thread and tie in the foam at midshank. Then wind back the thread to just beyond the hook bend, tightly compressing the foam. The rear-protruding foam will be pulled over later, wing case style. Tie in the peacock, and wind a plump abdomen. Tie in three strands of Krystal Flash® (spinner wing style), and separate the strands with wraps of thread to simulate three spread legs on each side. Pull the foam over, and secure it with several wraps of tying thread. Whip finish on the bare hook just behind the hook eye. Snip the foam leaving a small "head." Primp the legs to protrude horizontally in a spread-out manner. Trim the legs to length and cement at base of legs.

Another important beetle pattern is meant to be fished subsurface:

Black Glass Bead-Head Beetle

Hook: TMC® 2302—size 8

Thread: UNI-Thread®, black 6-0

Head: Black bead

Body: Chenille, large, black

Shell back: Hi Vis® "sheaf," black

Hackle: Turkey wing covert, large, gray

Tying Notes: Crimp the barb and apply the glass bead. Tie in Hi Vis®; wrap it to hook bend. Hi Vis® will be pulled over, wing case style, later. Wind chenille abdomen. Tie in and wrap one or two turns of turkey covert just behind the bead. Pull the wing case over and secure it. Apply 5-minute epoxy to the entire wing case to give a shiny appearance.

Fishing Notes:

The Black Foam Beetle often needs to be fished with an indicator dry fly and a fine tippet.

The Black Glass Bead-Head Beetle has taken some impressive brown trout when cast into the tail ends of riffles and washed into the pools, especially near the banks of wooded sections of streams, often as early as April (see Color Plate 15).

Ants are well known to the fly angler. Important to ant imitations are two separate bulges (abdomen and thorax/head) with a pronounced "waist." Also important is visibility. Lou Jiricowic's Pass Ant has proved to be excellent. Also note the Flashback Black Wet Fly, page 99.

Pass Ant

Hook: TMC® 102Y—size 19

Thread: UNI-Thread®, black 8-0

Abdomen, thorax/head: Foam, black
(a cross section approximately 1/8" x 1/8")

Hackle: Brown

Wing: Zelon®, white

Tying Notes: Crimp the barb and start tying the thread. Wrap to the hook bend, and tie a small abdomen of doubled-over foam. Take the thread to just behind the hook eye, and tie a thorax/head in a similar manner. Add a rather sparse Zelon® wing (just enough to allow visibility) at the waist, protruding back at 45 degrees. Then wrap two turns of size 18 hackle in front of the wing.

Fishing Notes:

In August, I have encountered situations in which the trout would not rise to 'hoppers or crickets yet confidently rise and sip the Pass Ant. This experience agrees with an observation by Walt Coaty that if the fish do not eat one kind of terrestrial, they will often take another. Be aware of the possibility, particularly in

September, that quiet water risers may be taking small dark-winged ants with very stubby legs. Use a size 18-22 Fur Ant tied with short hackle and a white "poly" wing.

Crickets and grasshoppers, again, are very familiar to the fly fisher. I continue to favor Tom Wendelburg's plump deer hair Black Cricket. The Hackle Wing Hopper still outfishes any other 'hopper pattern that I have fished. Both are well described in my earlier book.

"Grasshopper time" in the coulee country varies from year to year. In 1998 there were few 'hoppers, and the trout were not looking for them until early September, while 1999 produced large numbers of 'hoppers with good fishing by late July. Trout that are "turned on" to 'hoppers offer the most entertaining fishing of the year. To see a natural hit the water, give a few kicks and then to witness the take by an aggressive trout will definitely get your attention.

I consider 'hopper fishing as a "clinic on summertime holding water." The fishing is dynamic. Make one or two casts over likely spots, and keep moving. There is no need to make several casts over the same area. Do not be afraid to cast the line so that it drapes upon overhanging grass in front of you on your side of the stream. Use a tippet that can handle "weed eating" and the wind. Although grassy meadow streams are often best, especially on breezy afternoons, do not avoid the woods. Fishing 'hoppers at night may also produce desirable results.

Midge fishing continues through the summer months with the naturals generally being lighter colored and smaller than those of the cooler months.

Most streams have hatches of light cahills, and some streams have yellow stone flies. June is an important month for this activity, which fades later in the season. Imitations are well known. Spinner patterns for the light cahills can be important at times. Yellow stone flies may swarm over the riffles in the evening. Look for size 12 to 14 insects holding their abdomens extending upward. They might appear dark against the evening sky.

Tricos are a premier hatch on many coulee streams. Notable is the rarity of this insect on Wisconsin streams south of the Wisconsin River. Look for clouds of dancing spinners above the riffles, and fish a size 22 to 24 spinner pattern to sipping risers in the quiet water below. Hatching activity begins in July (the earliest I have noted is July 6) and continues into September.

Lower reaches of some of the large rivers support Isonychia species and Ephoron leukon. Look for action in August and September.

CHAPTER 10
LATE SEASON FISHING:
OCTOBER THROUGH DECEMBER

The fly fisher seeking salmonids has two choices during the late season: Fish the Great Lakes tributary streams for steelhead, brown trout and salmon, or fish the limestone spring creeks of Iowa. Most often I find myself on the spring creeks.

The spring creeks at this time of year are low and gin-clear, and the native trout are well educated. In October the display of autumn color on the bluffs and the migration of hawks and eagles along the Mississippi River are worth the trip (see Color Plate 16).

Various hunting seasons are now open. I have encountered duck hunters, squirrel hunters and bow hunters. As mentioned, remember to wear blaze orange while fly fishing (see Color Plate 16). Be aware of the possibility that you might be spotted by a hunter, especially when you are working quietly upstream with only your head in view above the crest of a bank or are sneaking around brushy stream bends.

Do not disturb native brown trout spawners near or on redds in late October and November. It is always gratifying to see three or four brown trout over 18 inches on redds. It gives you an appreciation for their survival skills and a hope for their reproductive success.

The main hatches of the period are the previously discussed Baetis, midges, tiny olives and terrestrials. Baetis hatch on gray, blustery days, generally in the afternoon. Use the various blue-winged olive patterns in size 20 and 22. Midges continue, as always. If you are not proficient at midging, a New Year's resolution to become a better "midger" might be in order. Tiny, flush-floating patterns are often most productive during this period for dimpling trout.

The tiny olives continue into November.

Trout do not forget terrestrials. The latest I have taken a brown trout on a 'hopper is December 4. Even without risers present, a BHP Beetle or Hackle Wing Hopper will produce—all day. Dimpling trout beneath trees in the fall may be taking size 20 Leaf Hoppers, imitated by pulling a wing case of 1 or 2 tan goose biots over an abdomen dubbed fluorescent green.

Chapter 10–Late Season Fishing: October Through December

Much fishing will be done beneath the surface with scuds, bead heads and other larva and nymph imitations. Stream channels in watercress are fun to fish with an unweighted red San Juan Worm. Cast the worm along the edge of a channel, and allow it to sink slowly and drift with the current. Often you will see the flash of the trout as it darts from under the cress to take the fly. Brown-cased caddis flies are common stomach contents of fall-caught fish. A Peeking Caddis or a Bead Head Pheasant Tail will work well. A 15-inch brown trout caught and released on the North Bear Creek "coughed up" a brown/cream sculpin (size 2). Minnow imitations and leeches are always in order.

My fishing year generally comes to a close in mid-December. I do remember the comment made by a guide on the Bighorn River in Montana. He noted that "On Christmas Day it is really nice—there is no one on the river."

CHAPTER 11
CONTRIBUTING EXPERTS

The idea for a chapter by contributing experts came from Iowa City, Iowa, resident Mike Hogue, owner of Badger Creek Fly Tying and a longtime fly fisher and contributor to the sport.

The opportunity to gain insights and include patterns of dedicated local fly fishers who are experts in the Driftless Area was too good pass by. All five experts contacted—Mike Hogue, Tom Dornack, Wayne Bartz, Walt Coaty and Tom Wendelburg—agreed to submit a few favored fly patterns and provide comments pertinent to fly fishing our streams.

Mike Hogue is an Iowa native and has been tying flies since the late 1980s. Many of his fly designs have appeared in regional and national magazines and books. He has served as a tying demonstrator, lecturer and instructor at regional workshops and National F.F.F. gatherings. Mike is the owner of one of the first Internet fly-tying catalogs and companies, Badger Creek Fly Tying. You may see his Web site at http://www.MWflytying.com.

Mike's Gold Demon

Hook: Kamasan® B401—size 14, 16

Thread: Black 8-0

Tail: Golden badger hackle fibers

Body: Fine gold holographic tinsel

Thorax: Peacock herl

Hackle: Golden badger

Tying Notes: This fly is a straightforward tie, tied in order of the listed components. The thorax is pronounced and covers the anterior one-third of the shank. Four or five turns of hackle are wound over the thorax.

Fishing Notes:

Mike notes that the Gold Demon is actually a cluster midge and is used during periods of heavy midge activity. It may also be used as a general searching pattern.

Mike's Gold-Stripe Hare's-Ear

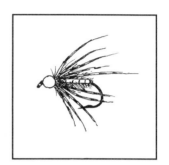

Hook: Mustad® 3906B—size 12, 14

Thread: Black 6-0

Head: Gold bead, 1/8"

Body: Mix: fox squirrel, 60%; hare's-ear dubbing, 20%; Lite Brite® pearlescent, 20%

Side stripes: Gold holographic tinsel, fine

Rib: Copper wire

Hackle: Partridge

Mike's Gold-Stripe Caddis

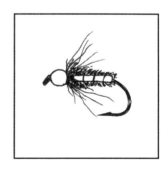

Hook: Mustad® 3906B—size 12, 14

Thread: Black 6-0

Head: Gold bead, 1/8"

Body: Hareline® crystal dub, peacock

Side stripe: Gold holographic tinsel, fine

Rib: Copper wire, fine

Thorax: Black squirrel

Tying Notes: For both Gold-Stripe flies, tie in the ribbing, then one 1¹/2" length of tinsel on each side. Dub the abdomen, pull the tinsel forward (like a lateral line) on each side and tie off; then advance the ribbing.

Fishing Notes:

Both of the "gold-stripes" are useful on all streams, year-round. Drift them through deep undercuts and the heads of riffles. Mike is enthusiastic about the "gold-stripe" design—"It definitely attracts large trout."

Tom Dornack lives in Eyota, Minnesota, and started fly fishing and fly tying in 1971. Tom has fished throughout the United States, but most of his time is spent on the spring creeks of southeast Minnesota. In 1973 he joined the Hiawatha Chapter of Trout Unlimited and is its current president. Since 1981 he has been the coordinator of the chapter's Habitat Improvement program, which has resulted in the restoration of over four miles of area streams. Tom is the chairman of the Southeast Minnesota Council of Trout Unlimited, serves on the state Trout Regulation Committee and is involved with the Whitewater River Joint Powers Board.

I have had the privilege of spending a day astream with Tom. We fished a catch-and-release section of the Middle Branch of the Whitewater River in an area of the chapter projects, then fished Trout Run out of Chatfield. My one recurring thought during our time together was, "Man, this guy is really good!"

Flashback Black Wet Fly

Hook: TMC® 3769—size 12-16

Thread: Black 6-0

Body: Rabbit fur, black

Overbody: Krystal Flash® strands, 12-20

Hackle: Hen hackle, black, 2 turns, slightly oversized for hook size

Tying Notes: Tie in the Krystal Flash® to be used later as the overbody. Dub a thick body; then twist the Krystal Flash®, pull the strands over the body and tie off. Tie in and wrap two turns of hackle, which should be two hook gaps in length. Grasp the hackles with the fingers, and pull back; then wrap the thread over the base of the hackle to hold the fibers, angling back a bit. Whip finish.

Fishing Notes:

Tom feels that the pattern represents "black terrestrials," beetles, crickets or ants. He fishes the fly from May through September. It is particularly useful on windy days with no apparent hatch. Most often the fly is fished deep, with added split shot 12 to 18 inches from the fly. Occasionally Tom fishes the Flashback Black Wet Fly in the film, especially if he notes sporadic risers. His largest fish on the fly has been a 20-inch brown trout. Tom prefers 2- and 3-weight rods for much of his fishing.

Inverted Hook Zonker

Hook: TMC® 300—size 2-10

Thread: Black or red 3-0 or 6-0

Weight: Dumbbell eyes sized to match the hook

Body: Chenille, olive

Overwing: Rabbit strip, black

Tying Notes: Tie in the eyes, Clouser style, on top of the hook, leaving enough room behind the hook eye to secure the chenille and rabbit strip. Take the thread to the hook bend, tie in the chenille, and advance the thread to the hook eye; then wind the chenille forward with a figure-of-eight around the eyes. Secure the chenille. Reverse the hook in the vise, and run the point of the hook through the rabbit strip, making sure that enough strip projects forward to tie off at the hook eye. The length of the trailing strip should be about the length of the shank. Pull the strip tightly forward (the pierced portion is anchored at the hook bend by the chenille), and tie it down.

Fishing Notes:

Tom feels that this fly is at its best following a rain with the water a bit off-color. Most often the retrieve is by stripping. Vary the speed of the retrieve as needed. Occasionally the fly is fished dead drift.

Tom notes that in 1999 he took six brown trout over 19 inches (the largest 24 inches) on the Inverted Hook Zonker.

Wayne Bartz has lived and fly fished in southeast Minnesota for most of his life. Currently he lives in Rochester, Minnesota. Wayne is a field editor for *Midwest Fly Fishing* magazine, and I have referred to his writing while researching this book. He also writes the Fly Tiers Exchange segment for *Midwest Fly Fishing*. For 12 seasons Wayne has guided on southeast Minnesota spring creeks.

Root River Special

Hook: TMC® 5262—size 12-16

Thread: Black

Head: Copper bead, $^1/8''$

Tail: Hen hackle, brown

Body: Fur dubbing, black with guard hairs

Hackle: Hen hackle, brown

Tying Notes: This tie is straightforward. Wayne prefers the copper bead to the brass bead. He uses tungsten beads for fast water. The hackle is palmered over the plump body.

Fishing Notes:
Although Wayne likes the Root River Special on all southeast Minnesota streams, he feels that it is particularly good in streams with stone fly nymphs—hence the name. Fish it dead drift.

Large trout are most often found in the depths; this is the zone of the bead-head.

P.G. Caddis

Hook: TMC® 102Y—size 15, 17, 19

Thread: Olive 8-0

Butt: Antron® dubbing, orange

Body: Peacock herl

Underwing: CDC dyed "wood duck gold"

Wing: Coastal deer

Tying Notes: This fly is tied in the order of the listed components. Use two CDC feathers. The wing should be slightly longer than the hook shank.

Fishing Notes:

Wayne says that this fly was developed to imitate egg-laying caddis. The pattern is useful during any caddis activity in the Midwest and in Montana. The imitation is also useful as a searching pattern. Wayne states, "This is the best all-around dry fly I use."

I had heard about **Walt Coaty** long before I met him. His name was mentioned in the Coon Valley area by local expert Dennis Graupe. At the Avalanche, Wisconsin, store, Roger Widner showed me flies tied by Walt. On Minnesota's Pine Creek, two local fly fishers asked me about Walt when they found out that I live in Wisconsin. When finally meeting Walt, I was happy to compare fly-fishing experiences on coulee area spring creeks. Our first conversation lasted for over three hours.

Walt lives in La Crosse, Wisconsin. He has been fly tying and fly fishing for over 40 years. He also builds cane and graphite fly rods. Although he spends a few weeks in the West each year, he does the majority of his fly fishing in the limestone spring creeks of Wisconsin, Minnesota and Iowa. He prefers fishing dry flies and matching hatches and is considered an authority on the hatches in our area.

Hendrickson Dun-Emerger

Hook: TMC® 100—size 14

Thread: Griffiths®, dark brown 14-0

Shuck: Zelon®, dark brown

Body: Caddis emerger dubbing, Hendrickson pink

Wing: CDC feathers, 2 short and dark gray (duck),
2 long and medium gray (goose)

Sulphur Dun-Emerger

Hook: TMC® 100—size 14, 16, 18

Thread: Griffiths®, light yellow—size 14

Shuck: Zelon®, dark brown

Body: Awesome Possum®, yellow

Wing: CDC feathers (as in previous fly)

Tying Notes: Tie in the shuck, and dub a cylindrical abdomen with a slight bulge in front. Place the two short CDC feathers back to back so that they flare outward, and tie them in at normal wing position, slanting back, the length to be just beyond the hook bend. Tie in the longer CDC feathers, one on each side, cupped with the short feathers flaring outward. The long wings extend to midshuck. Dub a thorax ahead of the wing; tie off.

Fishing Notes:

Walt says that this is a simple fly that really works. The Hendrickson Dun-Emerger is his mainstay fly for that hatch. (At times he uses a parachute pattern.) When the Hendrickson duns appear in midafternoon, Walt likes to be near the riffles and to look for a good fish. He casts about four feet above the fish, then pulls the fly under the surface, lets it drift about two feet and then lets it pop to the surface. He says that the fish respond immediately. He believes that 99% of the time the fish are taking emergers and that this pattern imitates them very well. At the end of the hatch, the Hendrickson Dun-Emerger is fished in the quiet water—without movement—to imitate crippled emergers.

The Sulphur Dun-Emerger is used in the same way and is especially good for the larger E. rotonda and E. invaria. In size 14, the pattern may be used as a light cahill.

Walt has been fishing this imitation in one form or another for over 20 years. He prefers 4- and 5-weight cane and graphite rods, 8 to 9 feet long.

I first became acquainted with **Tom Wendelburg** through his writings in national magazines. Whether he was writing about fly-fishing techniques or flies, his articles had direct application to my fishing. His article "Secrets for Luring Large Brown Trout" (see References) is perhaps the finest fly-fishing article I have read.

When I learned that Tom had moved from Montana to Madison, Wisconsin, I contacted him for a day of guiding. I learned more from Tom that February day than I had learned during the preceding five years.

Tom's fly designs have a well-earned national reputation. His All Marabou Leech and Hare's-Ear Scud will take large trout on any stream. They have become "most-used" patterns of my collection.

Tom fishes southwest Wisconsin's spring creeks regularly. His book about fly-fishing secrets for taking large trout will be published soon.

Trailing Shuck Baetis

Hook: Mustad® 94840—size 14-20

Thread: Olive 8-0

Shuck: Antron® yarn, gray

Abdomen: Rabbit underfur, brown-olive

Wing: Duck quill, slip from primary

Thorax: Same as abdomen

Tying Notes: Tom ties a thin cylindrical abdomen. The duck quill wing slips are tied one to each side, tip flaring outward and back, length to hook bend. The thorax is a slight bulge ahead of the wing.

Fishing Notes:
Tom notes that this imitation is very effective during the early stages of an olive hatch and is fished in the film. The pattern is not limited to olives and may be used for Hendricksons, sulphurs and more in appropriate colors and sizes. This pattern is fully discussed in Tom's article "The Duns of Autumn" (see References).

Sulphur Dun

Hook: TMC® 100—size 14, 16

Thread: Flymaster®, tan 6-0

Tail: Hackle, light ginger, split

Body: Mix hare's-ear, tan, fine, with a hint of rabbit, yellow

Wing: Wood duck flank, upright, split

Hackle: Light ginger

Tying Notes: The split wings are tied in first, just behind the thread head area. Tie in the split tail fibers; then dub a very thin cylindrical abdomen behind and ahead of the wing, and tie it off. Wind the hackle sparsely behind and ahead of the wing, and tie it off. Clip the hackle flat on the bottom.

Fishing Notes:

Tom feels that the clipped half-hackle image is important to the success of the fly during the E. invaria and E. rotonda hatch. He uses 6 or 7x tippet and a 2-weight rod. If the trout are extremely selective, go to the previously mentioned trailing shuck pattern tied as a sulphur.

REFERENCES

Geology of Wisconsin and Upper Michigan, Including Parts of Adjacent States, by Paull and Paull. Dubuque, Iowa: Kendall Hunt Publishing Co., 1977.

"A Tale of Two Waters," by Vince Marinoro. Outdoor Life, April 1976. This excellent article discusses the differences between spring creeks and freestone streams.

"Trout Fishing Regulations and Guide, Pub-FH-302," the Wisconsin Department of Natural Resources, P. O. Box 7921, Madison, WI 53707.

"Southeast Minnesota Trout Streams," map and current fishing regulations pamphlet, Minnesota Department of Natural Resources, Section of Fisheries, Box 12, DNR Building, 500 Lafayette Road, St. Paul, MN 55155.

"Trout Fishing Access in Southeastern Minnesota," Minnesota Department of Natural Resources, Section of Fisheries, Box 12, DNR Building, 500 Lafayette Road, St. Paul, MN 55155.

"Iowa Trout Fishing Guide," map, Iowa Department of Natural Resources, Wallace State Office Building, Des Moines, IA 50319-0034.

"Leaders for Selective Trout," by George Harvey. *Fly Fisherman* magazine, Spring Special, 1980. This article has influenced leader design for two decades.

Fly Fishing the South Platte River, An Angler's Guide, by Roger Hill. Boulder, Colorado: Pruett Publishing Co., 1991.

Practical Fishing Knots II, by Mark Susin and Lefty Kreh. New York, New York: Lyons and Burford, 1991.

"Trout Country, The Ecology of S.E. Minnesota's Streams and Rivers," by Thomas Waters. *Midwest Fly Fishing*, Vol. 4, issue 2.

"Aquatic Insects of Wisconsin. Keys to Wisconsin Genera and Notes on Biology, Habitat Distribution and Species," by William L. Hilsenoff. This pamphlet is a technical guide to aquatic insect identification and is available from any Wisconsin county extension office or by calling 608-262-3346.

References

"Blue Winged Olives, Get the Low Down Which Bug is it Blues?" by Dean Hansen. *Midwest Fly Fishing*, Vol. 5, issue 3.

Trout Fishing in Southeast Minnesota, by John van Vliet. Minneapolis, Minnesota: Highweather Press, 1992 and 1998.

Iowa Trout Streams, by Jene Hughes. Des Moines, Iowa: Second Avenue Bait House, 1994.

Exploring Wisconsin Trout Streams, by Steve Born, Jeff Mayers, Andy Morton and Bill Sonzogni. Madison, Wisconsin: University of Wisconsin Press, 1997.

Wisconsin and Minnesota Trout Streams, by Jim Humphrey and Bill Shogren. Woodstock, Vermont: Back Country Publications, 1995.

"Wisconsin Trout Streams," publication 6-3600(80), Wisconsin Department of Natural Resources, P. O. Box 7921, Madison, WI 53707.

"Midwest Fly Fishing," magazine, Tom Helgeson publisher, 4030 Zenith Avenue South, Minneapolis, MN 55410. Telephone 612-926-5128. Published 6 times yearly.

Borger Color System, by Gary A. Borger. Wausau, Wisconsin: Tomorrow River Press, 1986, 1995.

"The Geography of Wisconsin's Trout Streams," by C. W. Threinen and Ronald Poff. Wisconsin Academy of Sciences, Arts and Letters, Vol. 52, 1963, pp. 57-75.

"A Review of Trout Management in Southeast Minnesota Streams," by Thorn, Anderson, Lorenzen, Hendrickson and Wagner. North American Journal of Fisheries Management 17:860-872, 1997.

"Groundwater: Protecting Wisconsin's Buried Treasure," publication WR-224-89, Wisconsin Department of Natural Resources, P. O. Box 7921, Madison, WI 53707.

"1996 Trout Angler Survey on Public Trout Fisheries in Iowa." Project leader David L. Moeller, Iowa Department of Natural Resources, Wallace State Office Building, Des Moines, IA 50319.

Trout Stream Therapy, by Robert L. Hunt, Madison, Wisconsin: University of Wisconsin Press, 1993.

"Status of Southeast Minnesota Brown Trout Fisheries in Relation to Possible Fishing Regulation Changes." Staff Reprint #53, November 1997. Minnesota Department of Natural Resources, Section of Fisheries.

"A Toehold in the Kickapoo. A comprehensive management plan is gaining acceptance," by Jeff Mayers. Midwest Fly Fishing, Vol. 4, issue 2.

Catch and Release Guidelines: Federation of Fly Fishers Handbook, third edition, Bozeman, Montana.

"The Right Foot Forward: Change Your Stance to Improve Casting Accuracy," by Art Lee. *Fly Fisherman* magazine, Vol. 29, Number 1, December 1997, p. 62.

"Line Control: putting stripped line in its place," by E. Neale Streeks. *Fly Fisherman* magazine, Vol. 25, Number 1, December 1993, p. 46.

"Secrets for Luring Larger Brown Trout," by Tom Wendelburg. Fishing Facts, July/August 1990.

"The Movement of Trout," by Richard T. Grost, Trout magazine, Winter 1997.

"Status and Trends for Inland Trout Management in Wisconsin." Arlington, Virginia: Trout Unlimited report, 1999.

Upper Midwest Flies That Catch Trout and how to fish them, by Ross A. Mueller. Appleton, Wisconsin: R. Mueller Publications, 1995.

Trout Unlimited's Guide to America's Best 100 Trout Streams, by John Ross. Helena, Montana: Falcon Publishing Inc., 1999.

"The Phillips Usual," by Francis Betters. *Fly Fisherman* magazine, Season Opener 1980, p. 32.

"The Usual with a Twist, by Art Lee. *Fly Fisherman* magazine, Vol. 20, No. 1, 1989.

Nymphs and the Trout, by Frank Sawyers. Crown Publishers, Inc., New York, NY 1973 edition.

References

"Midwest Super Hatches," by Dean Hansen. *Midwest Fly Fishing*, Vol. 5, issue 2.

"Hatches of the Southeast (Minnesota)," by Wayne Bartz. *Midwest Fly Fishing*, Vol. 4, issue 2.

Caddis Super Hatches, by Carl Richards and Bob Braendle. Portland, Oregon: Frank Amato Publication, 1997.

"Two Flies Make a Summer," by Dick Pobst. *Fly Fisherman* magazine, September 1999.

Hatches II, by Al Caucci and Bob Nastasi. New York, New York: Nick Lyons Books, 1986.

An Angler's Guide to Aquatic Insects and Their Imitations, revised edition, by Rick Hafele and Scott Roederer. Boulder, Colorado: Johnson Books, 1995.

"How to Fish Dry Flies," by George Anderson. *Fly Fisherman* magazine, Vol. 18, No. 5, 1987.

"Spring Creek Tactics," by George Anderson. *Fly Fisherman* magazine, March 1995.

"The Duns of Autumn," by Tom Wendelburg. *Fly Fisherman* magazine, Vol. 17, No. 1, 1985.

"Troubleshooting the Cast," by Ed Jaworowski. Stackpole Books, Mechanicsburg, Pennsylvania. 1999.

"Trout Stream Insects," Dick Pobst. Lyons and Burford Publishers. New York, New York. 1990.

"The Essence of Fly Casting," by Mel Krieger. Videotape.

WEB SITES

IOWA DNR   www.state.ia.us/government/dnr/index.html

MINNESOTA DNR   www.dnr.state.mn.us

WISCONSIN DNR   www.dnr.state.wi.us

STREAM FLOWS   wwwdwimdn.er.usgs.gov

SATELLITE IMAGES   http://terraserver.com

TROUT UNLIMITED   www.tu.org

FEDERATION OF FLY FISHERS   www.fedflyfishers.org/

HAWKEYE FLY FISHING ASSOCIATION   www.commonlink.com/hffa

MIDWEST FLY FISHING   www.mwfly.com

FOX VALLEY CHAPTER TROUT UNLIMITED   www.vbe.com.heusers/fvtu.htm
   This is my home chapter's award-winning Web site. The links are excellent.

WEST FORK SPORTS CLUB   www.mwt.net/~westfork/index.html

WISCONSIN FLY FISHING PAGE   www.wisflyfishing.com/

INDEX

Bold type indicates complete pattern description.

Notes

stains noticed
03/31/16 KM

Notes